COLLECTING
LUCKY COINS, TOKENS, AND MEDALS

Rita Laws, Ph.D.

HOUSE OF COLLECTIBLES
NEW YORK TORONTO LONDON SYDNEY AUCKLAND

House of Collectibles and colophon are registered trademarks of Random House, Inc.

RANDOM HOUSE is a registered trademark of Random House, Inc.

This book is available for special discounts for bulk purchases for sales promotions or premiums. Special editions, including personalized covers, excerpts of existing books, and corporate imprints, can be created in large quantities for special needs. For more information, write to Special Markets/Premium Sales, 1745 Broadway, MD 6-2, New York, NY, 10019 or e-mail *specialmarkets@randomhouse.com*.

Please address inquiries about electronic licensing of any products for use on a network, in software, or on CD-ROM to the Subsidiary Rights Department, Random House Information Group, fax 212-572-6003.

Visit the House of Collectibles Web site:
www.houseofcollectibles.com

Library of Congress Cataloging-in-Publication Data

Laws, Rita, 1956-
    Collecting lucky coins, tokens, and medals : instant expert /
Rita Laws.
        p. cm.
    Includes index.
    1. Numismatics—Collectors and collecting. I. Title: Lucky coins, tokens, and medals. II. Title.

CJ89.L39 2006
737.075—dc22

2005052736

Printed in the United States of America

10 9 8 7 6 5 4 3 2 1

ISBN-10: 0-375-72096-0
ISBN-13: 978-0-375-72096-3

CONTENTS

To Adriana, Dominic, Madison, and the grandchildren
yet to come, for making me one very lucky grandma.

ACKNOWLEDGMENTS

My mother and children, especially Joaquin and Jamie, who looked out for the younger ones while I worked, have been very supportive of this project.

Beth Deisher helped me transition into numismatic writing in recent years and find resources for work in this field. For her aid, I am very grateful. Dorothy Harris, Mark LaFlaur, Oriana Leckert, and Lindsey Glass of Random House were quick with answers to every question I asked.

INTRODUCTION

Better an ounce of luck than a pound of gold.
—Yiddish proverb

Luck is a whimsy. Its existence cannot be proved or disproved, much less guaranteed. Nevertheless, millions of people all over the world own a lucky coin or two, and some people collect them. There are thousands of varieties within the major categories, only a few of which can be described here. The lucky coin collector has a lifetime of hobby fun to look toward and a legacy of centuries to enjoy.

Coins and related items have always been one of the nation's most popular collectibles. There are many reasons why people collect coins, including the following:

- for enjoyment
- because of nostalgia
- for the challenge
- for investment
- out of a love of history and art
- to learn more about other cultures
- to be able to act as a curator for their own small metallic museums

In addition to all of the reasons that people collect any kind of numismatic item, collectors of lucky coins also enjoy the added bonus of the good fortune itself. Lucky coins are a tangible expression of an intangible, a belief that better times are just around the corner. And some lucky coins are steeped in superstitious lore and legend and thus have fascinating histories not found with ordinary coins.

Luck is formally defined as the chance happening of a positive or a negative event or as good fortune, prosperity, or success. People like the word. It makes us smile. We often name our dogs Lucky. We use it as a compliment: "Wow, you have all the luck!"

Variations of the word *luck* are sprinkled throughout the American vernacular. People come into good fortune when they luck out or luck in, but need cash when they are down on their luck. If the luck of the draw is with you at cards, you are a lucky duck or a lucky dog. Some people hope to get lucky or catch a lucky break, we enjoy lucky streaks, and we wish good luck to others. A potluck supper is a meal thrown together from whatever is available. At one time, people who were extremely lucky were thought to have been born under a lucky star or to have made a deal with a demon for their devil's luck. Hard luck is bad indeed and may have been brought about by a jinx, hex, or hoodoo, the people or things believed to generate bad luck.

There are more people in America of Irish descent than there are in Ireland, so it is no surprise that many luck-related terms in our culture are Irish in origin. Because of Irish immigrant influences, we have the saying "the luck of the Irish" and the terms *shamrock, four-leaf clover, leprechaun, pot o' gold, shillelagh, Blarney stone, claddagh, St. Patrick's Day, wearin' o' the green*, and *lucky charms*.

Luck is a universal concept that can be and is viewed from many different angles. It can be described as a product of superstition or as a paranormal phenomenon, and it can be described in psychological terms or as a philosophical choice. Luck is linked to mathematics and statistics and also crosses paths with religion. Some believe that what others see as luck is really a heavenly blessing.

Superstition

Luck as superstition predates most major religions. It is an ancient belief system. It survives, in part, because human beings are superstitious by nature, although much less so today than in centuries past.

It is good luck's built-in motivation that maintains our personal superstitions. We are more likely to remember when our lucky charms worked than when they didn't. This is why famous athletes insist on wearing the same pair of lucky socks or shorts for every game, even after a loss. It is why Olympic runners go through the same set of movements before settling in at the starting line. It is why basketball players bounce the ball a certain number of times before a free throw. Similarly, we tend to thank our lucky talismans or charms when things go well for us, but to blame ourselves when things go wrong, thus continually reinforcing the power of our charms.

Aside from personal rituals, for most Americans, superstition is also a form of entertainment. Like our daily horoscope prediction, we give it our attention but many people don't take it too seriously. We can do silly things to avoid bad luck and to encourage its opposite, but we are not consistent. Some of these actions and beliefs make sense. (Walking under a ladder can be dangerous.) Others defy logic. (Why would black cats be any less lucky than cats of a different color?)

Religious Belief

Superstition and religion intertwine regularly. Halloween is just one example. It is a virtual celebration of superstitions, a secular tradition for costumed children to beg for candy at the doorways of pumpkin-festooned homes. This spooky feast began as the Christian holy day of All Hallows' Eve, the night before All Saints' Day. All Hallows' Eve evolved from the fall festival of the pagan Druids and was considered a sabbath for witches.

Superstition dies hard. Several early Catholic popes relied on their astrologers when making decisions. Astrology, or prediction based on stargazing, was not outlawed by the Catholic Church until the 1600s. And even when it was decreed at the Council of Trent to be a superstition, exceptions were made for agriculture, navigation, and medical doctors.

This casual hybrid of faith and fear is evident all around us. Is the major league baseball player who makes the sign of the cross as he comes up to bat saying a prayer, indulging a superstition, or a habit, or both?

Phenomenon

Luck as a mysterious force or a phenomenon of the paranormal is a popular modern idea. Some people believe that meditation and positive thinking attract good fortune like iron to a magnet. And once a person becomes magnetic, good things follow, especially in the areas of finance and romance. "Lucky in love" describes a personality saturated in a mystical attractiveness.

Psychology

If the famous Swiss psychologist Carl Jung is correct about the existence of a collective unconscious shared by all humankind, then perhaps a superstitious nature is a part of us now because it was a part of our distant past. Superstition is also connected to our recent history. In one sense, a lucky attitude harkens back to childhood, when it was easy to believe in anything and everything, even the monster that hid under the bed at night but was invisible to Mom and Dad.

Some psychologists study luck and so-called lucky people, too. They find that our expectations matter a great deal. If we expect to be unlucky, we often feel that way. If we believe that our luck is all good, our lives will feel luckier.

Perspective is important, too. Optimists look at a long line at the bakery and feel lucky that it is not a lot longer. Pessimists feel unlucky to have to be in a line of any size.

Richard Wiseman, a British psychologist at the University of Hertfordshire in England, has studied "lucky pennies." One hundred subjects were asked to carry a Victorian penny for one month and to keep a diary about their overall luck in areas such as health and finance. The researchers found no measurable difference in the lives of the study participants, but thirty out of the hundred felt luckier, and 70 percent asked if they could keep their lucky penny when the study ended.

The lucky coins created a type of placebo effect. The people carrying them felt more confident, secure, and optimistic, which in turn had a positive effect on their lives.

Wiseman concluded that luck is something that can be learned if we pay attention to four essential principles: create opportunities, think lucky, feel lucky, and deny fate.

Philosophy

Philosophical jokesters ask questions such as, "Is being superstitious bad luck?" and "Is a four-leaf clover lucky for a person who can't count?" They also question the luck inherent in any lucky coin that would fall through a hole in a pocket. But as humorous as such questions are, serious philosophers have studied luck, too, because philosophy is the study of fundamental beliefs.

Philosophy professor Nicholas Rescher at the University of Pittsburgh says that people can discourage bad luck through exercising common caution, buying insurance policies, studying the odds, and increasing knowledge. Having good timing and being alert and prepared will foster good luck by helping people grasp favorable opportunities. Rescher teaches that luck can never be fully controlled and that this is positive. He describes a world without luck as boring, a life without surprises. The random nature of luck, good and bad, gives life the spice that awakens the palate.

Mathematics and Statistics

Is luck just a matter of beating the odds? Mathematicians have long worked to explain at least some luck as statistical probability. For instance, the science of luck tells us that there is such a thing as a lucky streak, statistically speaking, but no one can predict with certainty how long any streak will last.

If you flip a coin many times, it will land on the heads side roughly half the time and on the tails side roughly half the time. But while flipping the coin, there will be "streaks" when it lands on the same side five, six, or even ten times in a row. Probability has no memory, so anything is possible, but the longer you flip, the more likely you are to come up with about half heads and half tails.

In a lottery, the sequence of 1, 2, 3, 4, 5 is just as likely to come up as 5, 4, 3, 2, 1 or any random group of numbers. So all numbers are equally lucky. The balls in the cage have no preference for one sequence over another. There are some forms of gambling, like poker, that require skill as well as luck, of course. But for gambling options that require no skill at all, like a lottery, mathematicians say it is safer to think of chance as a cold statistical reality instead of personifying it as "Lady Luck."

Luck is simply another word for *probability*, according to the math experts. For example, each time you have a lucky hand of cards, the odds diminish that you will remain lucky. Therefore, gamblers must use their reason and logic and remember that while lucky and unlucky streaks do occur, they must all come to an end.

Luck's Allure

In small amounts and when combined with common sense, superstition is harmless fun. Carrying a lucky coin in a pocket is not difficult, is not obvious, and is not dangerous, whether it works or not. And it may just make us feel a tiny bit more confident.

Someone once asked the Danish quantum physicist Niels Bohr why he hung a horseshoe above the front door of his house when he did not believe in luck. "I have been reliably informed," said Bohr, "that it will bring me luck whether I believe in it or not."

1

A HOBBY RICH IN HISTORY

If you don't get killed, it's a lucky day for anybody.
—Abraham Polonsky

When a child makes a wish and tosses a coin into a fountain, it is the continuation of a custom that has linked coins and good luck since ancient times. The ancient Greeks did the same thing, but their intent was to make an offering to the gods. In return for the money, it was hoped that the water would make and keep them healthy.

This custom is so strong even now that the smallest public fountain is likely to have a sprinkling of pocket change shimmering on the bottom. At zoos, signs have to be posted near alligator moats reminding people *not* to throw coins into the water because the alligators eat them and get sick.

The first half of the twentieth century was the heyday of American lucky pocket piece production, but lucky coins have been with us for much longer. In fact, coins have always been associated with religious belief and superstition. The first coins ever made came from the kingdom of Lydia (in modern-day Turkey) in the late seventh century B.C. From the beginning, these tiny sixteen-millimeter gold coins called "staters" were more than just a medium of exchange. They were a handy sacrifice for the gods, an investment, and a collectible.

The oldest lucky coins in Western civilization derived their luck through the consecrated monarchy or through religious symbolism. In the fifteenth century, British monarchs used "angel coins" to encourage instant cures. They waved them over the part of the subject's body that was broken or sick.

One hundred years earlier, the "touch coin" developed in France and England. A touch piece was an ordinary legal tender coin that had reportedly been handled by the monarch whose visage graced the obverse side. After the king or queen gave this coin to a subject, it was pierced and worn about the neck as both a lucky talisman and a symbol of prestige. The good fortune that supposedly flowed from a touch piece was quite specific. It was thought that certain diseases, such as scrofula, a type of tuberculosis, would be cured by wearing one.

Touch coins were popular for so long, they are surprisingly affordable today. Some that are for sale at online auction sites were recently found in Britain using metal detectors. They are usually well worn and, of course, holed. It is easy to imagine past owners rubbing small silver fourpence coins hung around their necks, hoping for improved health.

Touch pieces not only cemented the link between good fortune and coinage, they launched an industry. The practice of "wearing the king" eventually evolved into a fashion item called coin jewelry that remains popular to this day. In Victorian times, silver coins were brightly enameled and gold-plated. Later, they were carved into love token charms. Today, lucky coins and medals of gold, silver, and base metals can

be found in rings and on bracelets, necklaces, key rings, and brooches.

It was not a huge leap to move from a belief in the curative powers of a touch coin to a belief in a specific coin's predictive powers. This is what happened in 1658 when the very unlucky Cromwell Crown was struck in England.

Following the English Civil Wars (1642–51), Oliver Cromwell (1599–1658) was lord protector of England beginning in 1653 and ending in 1658, when he died of natural causes. As a king-substitute, his bust became the obverse design of a crown made the year before he died. The die producing this large coin soon developed a crack, called a die break, that created a raised line of metal in each coin. This line ominously ran horizontally across his neck. Many people

Some of the oldest examples of touch coins derived luck from the monarchy, including these two genuine British holed touch coins: (left to right) Charles II fourpence groat (1673) and James II groat (1686).

Some older lucky coins include (left to right) a modern reproduction of a gold British King Richard III angel coin (1483–1485) and a medallic copper replica of a gold Hungarian Kremnitz (1600–1800).

believed this foretold Cromwell's imminent beheading, and, strangely, they were correct.

After Charles II took back the throne in 1660 and eradicated the Commonwealth (a republic that temporarily replaced the monarchy), Cromwell's body was exhumed from Westminster Abbey, hung from a gallows, and then ceremoniously and publicly beheaded. The head was placed atop a tall pole at Westminster Hall, where it remained for many years. It reappeared in the 1770s and passed from one owner to another until the 1930s. It was X-rayed at that time, and the film clearly showed part of the stake embedded in the skull. In 1960 the head of Cromwell was given to Sidney Sussex College at Cambridge University, where it was laid to rest after three centuries.

The unlucky Cromwell Crown remains a popular collectible on both sides of the Atlantic. Recently, a gilded (gold-plated) example with the infamous neck-line die break sold at auction for almost $2,000.

In some cultures, gold is considered the luckiest metal of all from which to fashion coins. Even now, many of the wealthy keep a lucky gold coin handy. The gold ducats made at the Kremnitz, Hungary, Mint from 1600 to 1800 were considered particularly adept at deflecting ill fortune. Called Kremnitz coins, one side featured St. George slaying the dragon and the other, Christ asleep in a boat with his apostles during a storm. Translated, the legends read, "St George, Patron of the Knights" and "Safety in the Storm." Soldiers and sailors felt far more comfortable going into battle or sailing the sea with one of these in their pockets.

Over the past four centuries, St. George and his doomed dragon have appeared on the coins and tokens of many nations, including places as close to home as Canada, but it is the original two-sided design of the Kremnitz that is considered lucky. And these pieces remain popular. Today, copper Kremnitz tokens and medals are struck for those who don't wish to spend hundreds of dollars on the antique gold ducats. They are particularly popular among people with family members serving in the navy.

The Coin Collecting Bug

Coins and medals have been avidly collected for millennia. This has been called the hobby of kings because some specimens are so expensive, only royalty can afford them. But lucky coin collecting is a hobby for the rest of us. If you have a penny in your pocket, you've already begun your collection. Even the older coins are not necessarily expensive. For example, ancient Chinese lucky cash coins are readily available for a few dollars apiece, and some are two thousand years old.

Collectors talk about catching the "coin bug," because once this field grabs you, there is nothing to do but indulge the urge. And you will probably hope that at least one member of your family catches the contagion, because this is a great hobby to share with loved ones.

Of course, as with any hobby, expertise is essential in order to build a collection of any size and quality at a reasonable cost. To become an instant expert in coin collecting, one must first have the essential tools described in Chapter Two, especially an awareness of what factors make one coin more valuable than another. Next, the enthusiast needs an understanding of the major categories of coins, as described in Chapter Three. Reading this book is the first step and should be followed by purchasing a few coins through the offline or online resources listed in Chapter Four. And Chapter Five presents all of the lingo and acronyms any collector needs.

With each purchase, research the background of your coin as thoroughly as you can. This will not just raise your level of expertise; it will increase your enjoyment of this fascinating hobby. As funds allow, purchase a coin magazine subscription and a price guide or two. Join a coin chat on the Internet or a local coin club. Socializing and networking with other collectors is fun and profitable. You will be among others who understand your passion for coins, and you will be able to laugh and learn while sharing what you know with beginners.

A computer with a modem is not required, but if you have one, you are off to a fortunate start in this type of collecting. Thousands of coins and related items are available at various online auction sites, day and night. You can collect medals that contain lucky symbols (like shamrocks and horseshoes), tokens that specifically promise good fortune to their owners, genuine coins traditionally thought to be lucky, reproductions of famous lucky coins, hell notes (the lucky currency of the dead), and much more.

The only tough decision the lucky coin collector has to make initially is whether to specialize or gather a generalized collection. For the specialist, a few choices include

- lucky dragon coins of Asia
- banknotes with consecutive lucky 8s
- U.S. large and small cent types
- lucky pocket pieces made for children

- Chinese, Japanese, and Korean cash coins
- Austrian frog tokens
- Commonwealth sixpence
- elephant numismatics
- rolled and encased lucky coins
- military challenge coins
- angel coins from countries like France, Hungary, and Mexico

Most people begin building a general collection while they learn the basics of the hobby and then specialize later when a particular category or variety captures their interest. They might choose to finance the purchase of new acquisitions in their specialty by selling off items collected outside of the specialty.

Lucky Coin Rules

As children, most of us owned at least one lucky pocket piece. In this regard, Americans are not unique. Whether it's a charm, a talisman, an amulet, a coin, a medallion, or a token, people all over the world and throughout time have enjoyed carrying small objects with them that are said to bring good luck. The lucky coin is the most well known of these concrete symbols, followed by stringed beads, jewelry, and various types of clothing accessories, such as lucky hats.

Depending on where you live, there are certain unwritten guidelines or "rules" governing the acquisition and use of lucky coins. In the United States, you might hear the following:

- Pick up a penny you find in a parking lot, but only if the coin is "heads up."
- Toss a coin into every fountain or small pond you encounter and make a wish.
- Keep coins that are bent, as they are especially lucky.
- Keep coins with significant dates on them, such as your anniversary, birthday, or the birthdays of your children.
- Keep the first coin you ever earned.
- Never spend the very last coin in your pocket. ▣

2

THINK AND TALK LIKE A COIN EXPERT

We must believe in luck. For how else can we explain the success of those we don't like?

—Jean Cocteau

Lucky coin collectors can't rely on luck alone to build quality collections and avoid counterfeits. The traditional advice given to new coin collectors by old-timers is, "First buy the book." This means that to get the best deal on a genuine specimen, it is important to prepare ahead of time and to know something about the item. This applies to the lucky coin collector, as well.

Essential Knowledge

The key to the value of any coin or related item lies in knowing something about the following:

- its age
- its rarity
- its condition
- its history
- its metallic makeup

No one can look at a group of coins or medals and know which are the most valuable unless they have information about the age, rarity, and condition of the items. For example, a 1940 bronze large lucky Irish penny is worth six times as much as a 1928 Irish penny and fifteen times as much as a 1968 version in fine condition. The reason is mintage: 312,000 made compared to nine million and twenty-one million, respectively. The key date in the series is 1940, the year that Ireland minted the fewest of that particular type of coin. In this example, age matters because the 1928 is more valuable than the 1968, but rarity pushes the coin in the middle age group to the top of the price list.

Condition plays a big role, too. Fine condition means the coin has been circulated. In mint or uncirculated condition, the 1940 Irish penny is worth eleven times more than the 1928 coin and a whopping 150 times more than the 1968. Therefore, this particular coin's age is important, but it is rarity and condition together that are most crucial in determining market value. The lesson here is that collectors should always buy the finest-quality specimen they can afford now for maximum return later.

The history of a coin can also be an important factor in determining what it is worth. For example, a Lindbergh token that is pedigreed as having once belonged to Charles Lindbergh (also known as Lucky Lindy) or to a member of his family will be worth much more than a very similar item that has no documented history accompanying it.

Makeup refers to the metal that the coin, token, or medal contains. Obviously, silver, gold, or platinum items have a greater inherent value than common items made of copper, aluminum, tin, steel, zinc, nickel, brass, or bronze. The collector should never forget, however, that history, rarity, and condition can create an expensive collectible even from a humble aluminum token.

Common Vocabulary

The glossary at the end of this book defines the terms and abbreviations that collectors will encounter on their lucky coin hunts. A few terms are essential for all collectors to know up front. For example, *numismatics* is the study of coins, medals, tokens, medallic charms, and paper money, so it is a broadly used term. *Exonumia*, on the other hand, refers to those items of numismatic value that are not coins. This distinction is important because there is a major difference between coins and other related items: purchasing power.

Coins are legal tender and can be used to purchase something from any merchant within the country or state from which that coin was minted. Tokens serve many purposes, but they are never legal tender. Tokens may be exchanged for a specific service, such as a bus ride, but the token was purchased with legal tender (coins). Medals are commemorative in nature, honoring a person, a place, a thing, or an event. You can't use a medal to buy a loaf of bread, even if the medal is worth far more to a collector than a whole sack of groceries.

In addition to the meaning of *coin*, collectors should understand two other distinctions made by numismatists: the difference between a penny and a cent, and the difference between currency and paper money. *Penny* is actually a British term for one pence. The proper word for an American copper is *cent*.

Secondly, the word *currency* is often used by Americans to refer only to paper money. Collectors, however, define currency in its broadest sense, as legal tender, including coins and paper money.

Ironically, the term *paper money* has become outdated in recent years. In a time when foldable currency has to include sophisticated anticounterfeiting technology, the bill can have more linen or fabric than anything, and some countries now make banknotes out of durable plastic and vinyl.

Must-Have Tools

No special tools are absolutely required to collect a few lucky coins, but if you plan to enjoy this hobby for a long time, there are certain items that can save you a lot of money in the collecting phase and protect your investment for years to come.

The first thing you will need is a well-lit area within your home where you can view your lucky coins. The lighting is critical if you want to see details and be able to judge condition (grade) correctly. Look for the new lightbulbs that purport to mimic natural sunshine. These are available at most hardware stores and cost just a bit more than regular lightbulbs. For those who are really serious about minute, detailed examinations of the coins' surfaces, halogen lamps are often used by professional coin dealers because the light shows imperfections often not visible under ordinary lightbulbs. (Halogen lamps, however, should be used with care: it might be advisable to turn the lamp off when you're not using it to examine coins.)

Next is a magnifying glass or loupe. These are sold in varying powers (2x, 3x, 4x, etc.). For coins, 10x to 14x is really the lowest power recommended for viewing details. The higher powers are great, too. The more you learn about coins and medals, the more you will enjoy a high-powered glass.

If your magnifying glass sustains even the smallest of scratches, it can be very difficult to view your coins clearly. Choose a glass with a recessed lens so that when you set it down, the lens does not come into contact with your desk or table. If this is not possible, wrap your glass in a soft cotton cloth between uses to protect it from scratches and dust.

In a pinch, a good computer scan (one with a fine, high resolution) can substitute well for a magnifying glass. Simply scan the coin at 200 percent or more and you will see details on your computer screen that are not readily viewable by the naked eye.

It's impossible to maximize the spending power of your money when it comes to a collection if you don't know what to pay. A few good books are essential because the Internet won't offer all of the necessary information, especially in the area of detailed price lists containing tens of thousands of items.

Experts know that the up and down purchase price of coins and tokens is affected by many factors, some of which include:

The stock market
Generally speaking, when stocks are down, collectible coin prices are up, and vice versa.

The season
The best time to buy is during warm weather, and the best time to sell is during cold weather (people are more likely to spend time on indoor hobbies, like coin collections, during cold-weather months).

The spot price of gold, platinum, and silver (affecting only coins made of precious metal)
In 1980, when the price of silver went through the roof briefly, millions of silver coins and medals were melted that otherwise might not have been, creating a relative scarcity for certain types of world silver coins once considered common.

The discovery of a new "hoard"
The value of any rare type of ancient Roman coin, for example, will decrease at least temporarily after the discovery of a huge hoard of this same coin during an archaeological dig.

Publicity
When the state quarters found the limelight, interest in all types of U.S. quarters increased, which raised quarter prices overall.

Time
The value of virtually all coins increases over time as they become more and more scarce, but this is most significant with the finest examples of each type.

Because of fluctuations in value, a price guide is a very helpful tool. If you buy and sell frequently, you may need a new price guide annually or even monthly. The newspaper *Coin World* (*www.coin-world.com*) expanded their price list into a monthly magazine-sized U.S. coin guide called *Coin Values*, available at newsstands.

If your collection is growing slowly, purchasing a new comprehensive guide every three to five years is acceptable. With non-U.S. coins (called world coins by U.S. collectors), the most popular price guide is called the *Standard Catalog of World Coins* by Chester L. Krause and Clifford Mishler. It is revised annually.

New and used copies of the *Standard Catalog* are available at bookstores, coin shops, and online bookstores and auction sites. The publisher of the *Standard Catalog*, Krause Publications, also has a Web site, *www.krause.com*. Krause (pronounced KROU-see) sells guidebooks for other numismatic items, like tokens, Chinese cash coins, paper money, and ancient coins.

The *Standard Catalogs* are very thick and heavy. For collectors who prefer a more portable and economical alternative, there are the Blackbooks. The paperback *Official Blackbook Price Guide to World Coins* is small enough to fit in a purse. There are also Blackbook titles for U.S. coins and paper money. These are not as comprehensive as the Red Book and the Standard Catalog series, but they are a good start.

Some lucky coins are U.S. coins so a U.S. coin price guide can be very helpful. One that has been popular for many years is *The Official Red Book: A Guide Book of United States Coins* (or *Red Book*, for short), by R. S. Yeoman. It is published by Whitman–H. E. Harris (*www.whitmanbooks.com*).

Handling and Storing Coins and Tokens

Whether your collection is large or small, it is important to handle specimens carefully and store them in such a way that they are protected from humidity, dust, pollution, and excess light and heat.

Most people assume that handling a coin is harmless to the coin. But this is not exactly true. Human skin contains oil and moisture that adhere to the surface of the metal and, over time, affects its color. A single fingerprint left alone for several years will permanently mar a coin, even after it is wiped away. The gleaming shiny surface of a coin that has never come into contact with human hands can only stay perfect if it remains untouched.

The simplest solution is to wear cotton, plastic, or latex gloves when handling coins. These are quite inexpensive and can be purchased in small quantities or in bulk from stores that sell coin, cleaning, or medical supplies. You can also purchase plastic coin tongs (which you use for picking up coins) from any coin supply store. At the very least, try to handle your coins, medals, and tokens by gripping the edge only, not the front or reverse.

The storage method is important if you want to enjoy your coins and medals for a long time and especially if you view them as an investment. Metallic numismatic items should never be stored in a box where they come into contact with—and scratch—each other. These scratches, called contact marks, lower the coins' value. Also, a regular cardboard box will shed cardboard dust or particles. Over time, these will stick to the surface of a coin and cause the same kind of spotting and discoloration that fingerprints can make.

The proper way to store coins and medals is in plastic boxes after placing the items in individual hard plastic holders or *flips*. The flip is a dual-pocket holder with one side for the coin and one pocket for a small card on which you can write a description of the coin. It is a popular choice and comes in several sizes. Since two inches by two inches is the standard size for coin holders, these are often referred to as two-by-twos or 2x2 flips by collectors. There are three types of 2x2s readily available from coin supply dealers: vinyl, archival, and staple. Two of these are acceptable; one is not.

Vinyl 2x2s are inexpensive, but they are made from a soft pliable plastic that over a period of years will deteriorate. The product of this deterioration is a chemical ooze called polyvinyl chloride, or PVC. It shows up on coins as a sticky green film that is difficult to remove. Over time, PVC damages the coin's surface. Coins with this green goo are said to be PVC contaminated, and many buyers will not purchase them. Some soft vinyl 2x2s are safe to use for up to a decade before PVC develops, but since no one can be sure how long such a holder is safe, it is best not to use them at all.

Archival clear plastic 2x2s are more expensive and the plastic is more brittle, but these are safe for long-term storage. Since they are crystal clear, you can enjoy your token without ever removing it from the flip.

The least expensive safe method is the cardboard and Mylar 2x2, or staple-type 2x2. These are perfect for the beginning collector. These holders are cardboard squares with clear Mylar windows in different sizes. The coin is placed inside, and the holder is folded over it and then stapled shut. (There is also a more expensive variety that comes with a press-and-stick adhesive already applied.) Three or four staples seal this little holder against the dangers of the outside world. They are not airtight, but they definitely restrict air flow and therefore the damage that airborne moisture and dust can cause.

If possible, invest in a flat staple stapler. There are some easy-to-use electronic models that have anti-jam features. These are available at coin supply houses and office supply stores. These staplers flatten the ends of the staples as they close the holder. The traditional rounded end staples can damage the holder pressed up against it or scratch the Mylar. Flat staples eliminate this problem and also save space so that you can fit more holders into a storage box.

A flip discourages air circulation but cannot eliminate it, so there is a 2x2 nonflip option that protects the coin within clear hard plastic and never lets in air. These are called plastic holders or snap holders because two squares of hard plastic must snap together to seal the coin inside. Even though the outside dimensions of these hard plastic holders are two inches by two inches square, the inside dimensions vary with the size of the coin. So you will probably want to purchase a box of mixed sizes, penny to dollar size. These are made by companies like Intercept, the publisher of *Coin World*, and Whitman, among others.

Paper money should be stored in currency sleeves or top loaders. To avoid problems with PVC, look for clear semi-brittle plastic sleeves or those marked as safe for long-term storage. Top loaders are hard plastic cases open at one end for collectibles like baseball cards and comic books. It is more difficult to insert large-size paper money into a top loader, but they do provide excellent protection and, like world currency, come in a wide variety of sizes.

A low-cost alternative available at office supply stores is the sheet protector. These are three-hole punched clear sleeves designed to hold and protect documents in binders. Those marked archival safe and designed for long-term storage will work well for folding money. Place only one banknote into each protector so that they do not rub against each other. Place stiff sheets of paper or cardboard in between the sheet protectors as you place them into a binder. This will allow the money to lie flat.

Boxes or Binders

Once your coins, tokens, and medals are encased in flips or in Mylar or plastic holders and your paper money is securely stored in good quality currency sleeves, it is time to decide how to display them. The two main display options are plastic row boxes called *stock boxes* or clear vinyl pocket pages that fit inside a standard three-ring binder.

Using boxes allows you the opportunity to handle each holdered coin individually and to refile them quickly and easily. Plastic pocket pages are convenient because you can view your collection as easily as turning pages. Some collectors like to have several binders for different types, such as for lucky coins, lucky tokens, and lucky medals.

Try to avoid wood and cardboard boxes. Certain types of woods bleed oils that can damage coins that are not in airtight holders. And cardboard sheds particles that can spot coins over a long period of time. The best coin boxes are metal, plastic, or plastic-coated cardboard. Metal boxes should be rust free and treated to prevent rust from forming.

Coin Folders and Albums

In the United States, options for storage of same-size coins, such as hobo nickels, include folder and album. The common coin folder is a trifold or quad-fold piece of cardboard with die-cut depressions for the cents, nickels, or other designated denomination. More expensive but also safer are porthole albums, where coins are popped into openings and then protected on both sides by archival quality plastic strips that slide into the cardboard rows.

Most folders and albums accommodate only one size of coin, but lucky coins come in all shapes and sizes. Albums designed for *type sets* or *world coins* will have portholes of different sizes. A type set is a collection made up of one of each type of coin, such as one of each major type of U.S. coin made (small cent, large cent, two cent, etc). World coins, in the U.S., is a phrase that refers to all non-U.S. coins.

Another option is the European-type coin album. Coin collectors in Europe and Australia have long used albums that are made up of different size clear pockets made of safe long-term plastic. These pockets may have splits or pocketed slides or small flaps that fold over to keep the coins inside. No holders are required. Simply place your clean coins, tokens, and medals into the corresponding size pocket, and fold the flap over and inside. Quick and easy.

These European-style storage systems are not appropriate for circulated coins because over time, the dirt, oil, and moisture on these items will cloud the clear pockets, and they are very difficult to clean. For uncirculated items, however, this is a wonderful option. These albums are not always easy to find in the United States, but a large coin supply house would have them or know how to order them. See Chapter Four for information and resources concerning the purchase of archival-quality coin supplies of American and European manufacture.

Safe Storage

Whether you use binder or box, folder or album, avoid extremes of light, heat, and moisture in storage. The best rule of thumb is to store your collection where you would feel most comfortable enjoying it. A garage, for example, suffers from fluctuating humidity and temperature. This is bad for metal items and worse for paper money. Your collection is more delicate than you might think. Any environment with central heat and air-conditioning and low humidity is ideal.

Always check on your collection regularly, at least twice a year, especially if you live in a humid climate. If something in the air (such as moisture or smoke) is damaging your coins, you will want to catch the problem as soon as it starts. Dehumidifiers in humid places and good quality filters on furnace and air-conditioning systems will create a healthy atmosphere for collectibles.

If you keep valuable coins in a bank vault or safe deposit box, it is a good idea to place a few moisture-absorbing silica packets in the box, too. And check on your coins regularly. There have been reported instances of people storing items in safe deposit boxes that were harmed by gases emitted from other boxes. In one instance, a collector's paper money was damaged because a small hot pepper spray canister stored in a nearby safe deposit box developed a tiny leak that went unnoticed for months.

Living in the nation's tornado alley or hurricane belt brings with it the additional concern of what to do with a collection when Mother Nature loses her temper. You can take a very small collection along with you to the safe place you move to, but it is impractical to move a larger group. Happily, there is an alternative available that addresses this problem and that did not exist just one generation ago: the storm closet.

In the Midwest, outside tornado shelters or "fraidy holes" can range from a wood-braced hole in the ground covered with a heavy metal door to a concrete bunker several steps below the surface. Since these are small, difficult to enter, and not climate controlled, they are not conducive to collection rescue or storage. Modern in-home storm closets, however, are just about perfect.

An in-home tornado shelter or closet is made of steel-reinforced concrete or thick metal and is designed to withstand the three hundred mile-per-hour winds that accompany severe tornadoes and hurricanes. They can be installed in many types of existing homes and are almost standard in new housing in high-risk areas. Commonly, the storm closet will be modified for use as the walk-in closet in the master bedroom or as a utility closet on the ground floor. If you store your collection in the storm closet, you won't have to give it a second thought during severe weather. Your collection will already be safe.

Cleaning and Restoring Lucky Coins

We tend to think of metal as strong and damage resistant. After all, the shields of old that protected foot soldiers from spears and arrows were made of metal. When it comes to coins, however, collectors know that metallic surfaces are quite delicate.

When a coin is struck, the resulting sheen and shine from the coin die, the glow of the new coin, is called luster. Luster is the look of a new coin that cannot be duplicated by any other means known at this time. Once a coin is touched, circulated, or cleaned, luster is gone or at least is compromised, along with some of the coin's value. For this reason, collectors of mint-state and proof coins in perfect condition shudder at the thought of touching a coin with bare hands, much less cleaning it with chemicals.

If your lucky item is potentially valuable, no matter what its condition, it is wise to ask a professional for help before you do anything. You can visit your local coin shop or look for coin restoration ads in periodicals like *The Numismatist*, *COINage*, *Coin World*, and *World Coin News*.

Loss of luster is not likely to be a common concern of the lucky coin collector, however, because so much of this material was made long ago. The first half of the twentieth century was the "golden age" of lucky to-kens and medals. And since most lucky pocket pieces were carried in, well, pockets, their mint luster was gone long ago. Cleaning a dirty coin, if done carefully, will not damage it further and will make it more at-tractive.

Safe Cleaning

There is a right way and a wrong way to clean a circu-lated coin or token. The wrong way is to use industrial-strength metal cleaners. The right way in-volves pure substances and patience.

Many coin collectors will soak coins in plain water for several hours or soak dirty or stained coins in olive oil overnight. The key for a truly clean coin is to use dis-tilled or purified water, at least for the final rinse. Tap water, especially if it is hard water rich in minerals, will leave deposits behind as the coin dries. This can make the surface appear streaked or cloudy. Distilled water leaves nothing behind.

The best way to dry a cleaned coin is to air-dry on clean paper towels or a cotton towel. A handheld hair dryer can also be used. Once completely dry on both sides, the coin can be placed into a holder. Be certain that it is very dry or the tiny amount of moisture that remains will encourage mold growth inside the holder.

If water or olive oil is insufficient to remove all of a coin's grime, there are several commercial cleaning agents available that have been designed just for coins and medals. Two examples include MS 70 In-dustrial Strength Coin Brightener and Blue Ribbon Professional Coin Conditioner and Preservative. These and similar products are available at coin sup-ply outlets.

For a particularly stubborn problem, you can re-search it at a search engine, such as Google (*www.google.com*). Typing in a search term such as *cleaning coins* will net you hundreds of articles to read. Some of this information is helpful and some of it is questionable. *Caveat emptor!*—buyer beware! If you have doubts about your safety, don't go forward. If you are concerned for your coin, try testing the cleaning solution on a low-value coin from your pocket change. Be sure to use proper ventilation and gloves, too.

Some people swear by substances like vinegar, ammonia, alcohol, petroleum jelly, acetone (nail polish remover), naval jelly, lemon juice, and commercial lime and rust cleaners. No one can predict how any cleaner will react to every coin, so if you decide to try any of these substances, use test coins you can afford to lose. Remember never to mix the cleaners together as this can create toxic gases.

When Not to Clean Coins

It is only logical that mint-state coins, proof coins, and potentially valuable coins, medals, and tokens in any condition should never be cleaned without an expert's help. To do so could be a costly mistake. Even an innocent-sounding action like rubbing a dirty coin with a rubber pencil eraser can be harmful to a coin's surface, as can be seen when viewed under a magnifying glass.

There is one other type of coin that should almost never be cleaned. This is the humble cash coin, the old penny equivalents of China, Japan, Korea, Vietnam, and other Asian nations. Cash coins are easy to spot because they are round on the outside and have square holes in the middle. They constitute a major area in coin collecting and in lucky coin collecting. All cash coins are thought to bring good fortune.

Collecting cash coins is fascinating due to the extremely high number of types, some of which are one to two thousand years old! These donut-shaped coins are so common in certain varieties that you can buy a handful of three-hundred-year-old coins for a few dollars. On the other hand, many coin collectors don't take the time to learn about these coins and can miss rare mintmarks, dynasties, and bosen coins hiding among the more common types. This is one reason why you should not clean cash coins—you may have something valuable and not know it!

The second and most important reason why cash coins should not be cleaned is that to do so is tantamount to destroying their character. Ancient coins that are hundreds of years old will develop unique and sometimes very beautiful patinas.

The *patina* is the look of the coin, the surface variations and color of a coin. Cash coins made of common alloys of iron, copper, and bronze develop patinas that can be bumpy or smooth or both and will contain small amounts of various colors or color combinations (e.g., yellow, orange, black, brown, gray, red, and green).

A green patina, for example, is considered quite desirable. An uninformed collector mistaking this for PVC contamination could ruin the patina by cleaning the coin. Cash coin collectors would see a coin cleaned of its patina as the rest of us might view a badly damaged painting.

Rust Is the Exception
Iron coins and especially cash coins that are made mostly of iron can become quite rusty. Rust is not good for a coin or its patina. Rust consumes metal and will eventually leave small holes in the item. Some collectors recommend removing rust with commercial rust-removing agents. Others say the rust should only be removed by a professional coin restorer. Again, if you want to remove the rust yourself, practice on something you can afford to lose first, and always follow label instructions.

Counterfeits
Once you are set up for viewing your coins, and you have the means to store them safely and to clean them when needed, the next "tool" is the knowledge to protect yourself from fakes.

Detecting Counterfeits
Counterfeit coins, medals, and tokens are everywhere. Most are pretty simple to spot, but some are so good they fool most people, so all collectors should know a little something about the art of counterfeit detection.

Recently, a friend of mine who has never collected coins conveyed an experience she had with a counterfeit twenty-dollar bill. She has worked in a bank for about a year and has handled quite a lot of cash in that time. A regular customer handed her a twenty and asked for two tens. As soon as she looked at it, it was as if an alarm went off in her head. There was something about this note that did not look quite right. The color was okay, the paper felt good, and the letters, numbers, design, and president all looked technically perfect. But she was sure it was fake anyway.

Her supervisor tested it and confirmed what they both suspected. It was phony, and a good fake at that. The customer who brought it in was cleared of any intentional wrongdoing, and last she heard, the authorities were still on the trail of the phony bill's original source.

My friend could not tell me how she knew the bill was no good, but when you handle a great deal of any type of object, you unknowingly become a visual expert on that item. Working in a bank has transformed my friend into an excellent counterfeit currency detector. She doesn't have to explain how she instantly knows that a phony is a phony. What matters is that she can do it.

Over time, all coin collectors experience something of the same transformation. Without realizing it, they become so good at examining the real thing that when a fake comes along, it sticks out as obvious. The challenge is spotting the fakes when you do not yet have coin experience.

The first step is to pay attention to your initial reaction. If anything about a coin you wish to purchase makes you wary, don't buy it. If you already own it, compare it to a similar item that you know to be authentic. Use a magnifying glass and pick out several details on the coin or token to compare closely.

Next, compare the weight (if you own a postal scale or any device that can weigh small items) against the true weight listed in the coin price guide. Then compare the size and the thickness to the dimensions of the real thing. Look at the edge. Is the collar of the coin an even thickness? If it is a reeded edge, are the reeds straight and evenly spaced?

Be careful not to damage the coin while investigating it. If you scratch the surface of a gold coin because you suspect that it is gold-plated and it turns out to be solid gold, you've just permanently damaged a gold coin and lowered its value.

If you want to know whether a coin is silver or gold through and through, visit a pawn shop. They have ways to test coins and jewelry without damaging them and will often test your item free of charge. These gold test kits are also available for sale from some coin supply stores.

If you discover that your coin is fake and it is a U.S. coin, you should request a refund. If you believe the seller knew it was phony, he or she should be reported to the authorities. A federal law called the Hobby Protection Act makes it a crime to make or sell unmarked replica U.S. coins or paper money. Copies must be clearly stamped or marked with the word *copy* somewhere on the coin or banknote.

The illustration on the next page shows two lucky South African sixpence from the 1930s. The British king is seen on the obverse. One of these sixpence is a fake. Can you see any of the eight major differences?

The one on the right, though showing more wear, is the genuine coin. The counterfeit is actually slightly smaller than the real thing and weighs less than it should. The edge is too thick, and there are not as many reeds (vertical lines) on the reeded edge as there should be. The inside edge of the coin's collar is bent and uneven. The silver content is wrong, and the king's face lacks certain details when viewed under a magnifying glass. The date helps, too. The fake is a 1930 sixpence, a key date year when relatively few sixpence were made. No one makes counterfeit coins with common dates that are less valuable.

Avoiding Counterfeits
A coin buyer who was cheated once when he bid on the lot of "Twenty-Five Large Coins" at the online auction was not a novice—he had several years of expe-

rience. He did his homework. He checked out the seller, who lived an ocean away, and found that he had nearly perfect feedback (a list of the scores and comments from past customers). This seller sold computer parts; this was his first and only coin auction out of the three hundred auctions he had successfully completed.

Which lucky sixpence from 1930s South Africa is the counterfeit?

The photo was taken from a distance, but the buyer could see what looked like large silver crowns of the type that were popular worldwide throughout the 1800s and the first half of the twentieth century. One in particular caught his eye. It appeared to be a very rare crown of New Zealand, worth thousands of dollars. He e-mailed the owner to ask where he had obtained the coins. The reply? The seller had bought them from a live estate sale—in New Zealand!

The buyer put in his bid at the last minute and won the lot for $500. He wired the money, and the coins arrived three weeks later. He knew instantly that they were all fakes, every last one. They were poor quality counterfeits, too. One of them even had misspelled words on it.

Since the online auction site prohibited the sale of counterfeits, the buyer was confident about getting a refund. But the seller refused. Eventually, the seller was kicked off of the auction site for refusing to refund. The Web site eventually refunded $175 to the coin dealer, the site's maximum fraud claim amount. The buyer never did recover the rest of his money.

Perhaps the best way to avoid buying counterfeit coins in the first place is to buy from people you trust who also have experience with coins and medals. When you buy online, refuse to bid blind. If you see an auction for high-end numismatic items but the scans and photos are fuzzy or small, be very careful! You are bidding for items you can't see clearly, and you might be buying fakes.

On the other hand, bidding blind for inexpensive tokens and medals is a much more low-risk activity. They cost less than coins to begin with, and except for a relatively few rare and valuable specimens, such as Indian peace medals and certain Civil War tokens, they are rarely counterfeited. The profit potential lies in passing bad legal tender coins and banknotes. Tokens and medals just aren't profitable for the criminal. As long as the bidding doesn't go ridiculously high, chances are good you will be happy with your inexpensive token group. ◼

3

LUCKY COINS, TOKENS, MEDALS, AND PAPER MONEY

Fortune brings in some boats that are not steered.
                              —*William Shakespeare*

The history of lucky coins and related items is best told in the items themselves. In this chapter, the collector will find information about specimens from the United States and from around the world. Many people begin a collection without any specialty in mind. This works well because it exposes them to a wide variety. Sooner or later, a certain type of lucky pocket piece will probably capture the collector's interest like nothing else. A specialty is born.

The United States of America
Americans collect many things. Among the most popular are coins, stamps, sports cards, comic

books, dolls and action figures, books, art, and antiques. Within the coin collecting hobby are major categories, like U.S. coins, world issues, tokens, medals, and paper money.

Collecting lucky pocket pieces and related items runs the gamut of categories. These come in all sizes, shapes, and metals. The most common, well-known, and beloved of these is the humble lucky penny.

The American Lucky Penny

When large cents became too expensive to produce in the 1850s, the U.S. Mint designed a smaller version. While all types are popular with collectors, Lincolns are probably the most collected coin on earth. Among the reasons are these:

· They are said to be lucky.

· They are inexpensive to collect.

· There are millions of them because it is such a long-running series (since 1909).

· There are many interesting and some rare varieties.

· America is one of the world's most popular tourist destinations, and visitors take these copper coins back home with them.

· Finally, Abraham Lincoln is a greatly loved American icon, so anything associated with him will be collectible.

U.S. cent collectors point out that *penny* is actually a British term. *Small cent* is the proper name for the lowest denomination American coin. The word *small* is used to discriminate between the first cents made in this country, which were about the size of quarters.

They are called large cents. Cents shrunk to their current size with the short-lived flying eagle small cent, the predecessor of the beloved Indian head small cent.

It is doubtful, however, that Americans will ever stop saying "penny" or that they will ever consider any other U.S. coin to be luckier than the copper. Most Americans know this children's rhyme well:

> Find a penny, pick it up, and all the day you'll have good luck.

But are all Lincoln cents automatically lucky? Some people will tell you that they are lucky only if found face up, with the Lincoln side showing.

Indians and Wheaties

Before 1910, the Indian head cent was the nation's lucky penny. The person wearing the American Indian headdress is actually the mythical Lady Liberty, whose visage graced many early coinage denominations. "Indians" are a very popular collectible today. Even though they were not made after 1909, they still circulated up to the 1960s. Today, the more common dates in average circulated condition can be purchased for a dollar or two apiece.

Wheatie is a term of endearment for the Lincoln cents made up through 1958, the ones with the wheat stalk reverse. Since wheaties show up infrequently in pocket change nowadays, many people consider them especially lucky when they do find them.

Of course, the current form of the Lincoln—the one with the Lincoln Memorial reverse—has its fans, too. Penny fanciers will tell you that this reverse makes our American penny very special indeed. It is one of the few coins that can claim to depict the same person on both sides. If you look carefully at the Memorial side, you will see a tiny statue of the famous president seated in the center of it.

The Luckiest Lincoln Pennies of All

A penny is worth, well, a penny, right? Not necessarily. Since so many people collect coins, and specifically, Lincolns, the scarcer dates are worth much more than a common or recent date. Depending on condition, there are several date and mintmark combinations that are worth thousands of times their face value, a feat unmatched by any other coin denomination.

It is helpful to know which dates are considered rare and are therefore the most valuable. The list that follows describes a few. If you find one of these dates in your pocket change, you are extremely lucky.

These values were derived from a recent *Coin World*'s *Coin Values* guide. They are much less specific than what you find in the publication, meant here to be a general overview. Values do change over time, of course. You can find up-to-date prices and more than a dozen different categories of coin condition in the latest issue, available at *www.coinworld.com* or any newsstand.

Lincoln Date/ Mintmark	Condition	Average Value
1909-S VDB	Worn	$475
	Average Circulated	$700
	Like New	$1,200
1909-S	Worn	$65
	Average Circulated	$150
	Like New	$275
1911-S	Worn	$15
	Average Circulated	$25
	Like New	$145
1914-D	Worn	$125
	Average Circulated	$300
	Like New	$1,300
1931-S	Worn	$45
	Average Circulated	$65
	Like New	$90

The letters following the dates in the preceding list can be found in two different places on the Lincoln side of the cent. One exception is that the very tiny initials *VDB* (for the coin's sculptor, Victor David Brenner) are at the bottom of the reverse, or wheat stalk, side of the 1909 coin, if they appear at all. (A magnifying glass will help you to spot them.) After 1909, the initials disappear until 1918, when they regain their position (this time below Lincoln's bust) permanently.

The mintmark is a letter, such as *D* or *S*, that appears next to the date, which is to the right of the president's bust. These letters denote the mint where the coin was struck (e.g., *D* for Denver and *S* for San Francisco). The lack of a mintmark with small cents means the coins were struck at the Philadelphia Mint.

Penny Myths and Errors

Have you heard the myth about the million-dollar silver penny? Sadly, such a penny doesn't exist. Some penny myths are based in fact and the collector should be aware of them. Others are pure fiction.

The million-dollar silver penny rumor derived from the famous 1943 penny, or steelie. This was a war year, and the military needed all of the copper it could get. So the mints struck pennies that year, and that year only, out of zinc-plated steel. So many were made that even in like-new condition, today's value is only about $2 each.

The rumor about the million-dollar cent grew out of the fact that the mints also made a few 1943 copper pennies and a few 1944 steelies by mistake. These are extremely rare and valuable, so the odds of finding one are astronomical. The bogus rarities are still circulating among us. Beware. It is not difficult to copper-plate a 1943 cent or zinc-plate a 1944 date!

Which brings us to an important point for every coin collector to remember: *if a coin looks weird, it could be valuable.* Coins that contain mistakes generated at the mint are called error coins and are sought after by error collectors. More than a few Americans have thrown away a "damaged" penny not realizing it is a rare mint error. The challenge is to distinguish the mint error from the coins that are damaged after they leave the mint. Unfortunately, a coin that has been run over by a train or shot with a BB gun is not an error coin and is less valuable for its damage.

Among the mint errors are coins struck off-center, or without their collars. The more off-center the coin, the better. And if the off-center coin has a readable date, you have a very lucky find. Error collectors prefer coins with at least the last two numbers of the date intact.

The rarest and most valuable errors are doubled-dies and mules. A doubled-die Lincoln may look blurry at first glance because the die struck it in such a way that some of the design is doubled. The more obvious the doubling, the more valuable the coin. They can sell for $50 and up into the thousands. The most common dates for doubled-dies are 1917, 1955, 1969-S, 1970-S, 1972, 1983, 1984, and 1995.

Just as mules are the offspring of a horse and a donkey, a mule coin is derived from two totally different denominations of coin. And if the mint where the mule is struck also manufactures coins for other nations, the mule may have two sides from two different countries! Mules are spectacular and rare and highly collectible. Such a mistake is not common, and when it does occur, the mint usually catches it and destroys the errors before they enter circulation. But a few mules do get through.

The Sacagawea/Washington quarter mules first showed up in 2000. At first glance, one looks just like any other golden dollar, except that the reverse has the Washington side of a quarter, not the bald eagle. Only a few dozen at most escaped the mint, and experts believe most have been found, but not all. If you are lucky enough to find a genuine mule (as opposed to a counterfeit hybrid) in a roll of coins or in your change, wrap it in a clean cloth to protect it from scratches and get it appraised by an expert. If it's genuine, you have a very valuable find.

Lucky Aluminum
Aluminum is the most inexpensive metal from which a coin can be struck. For years, many nations have struck their penny equivalents from aluminum. It is ironic then that what may be the most valuable Lincoln cent of all is one made of aluminum. The problem is that it may not be legal to own it if you do come across one. Some legal minds hold that the few aluminum cents still unaccounted for are actually U.S. Mint property and subject to confiscation by the government.

The story of the aluminum cent begins in the early 1970s. At that time, the U.S. Mint began experimenting with different metals and alloys to find a more cost-efficient penny. The price of copper has risen so much that since 1982, all U.S. pennies have been copper-plated zinc, not solid copper. One of these experiments—or pattern coins, as they are called—was a group of Lincoln cents made from aluminum.

To test the acceptance of such coins, U.S. Mint officials gave an aluminum penny to each member of Congress. The idea fell flat. No one wanted an aluminum penny because it looked strange and felt too light. Later, U.S. Mint officials decided to gather up the patterns before they created a collector's frenzy, and most of them were taken back. Some politicians, however, had thrown their experimental pieces away or given them away, thinking of them as novelties or samples, not potentially valuable rarities. One congressman is said to have tossed his silvery-colored cent to a Capitol police officer as a token of appreciation.

One of these rare and unusual pattern coins surfaced in 2005. The U.S. Treasury Department has not yet decided whether to confiscate the coin. If allowed to retain it, the lucky owner could probably realize more than a million dollars for the coin at auction.

Altered Coins

An altered coin is simply a legal tender coin that has been purposely altered in some fashion by an individual or a commercial enterprise. The most common alterations today are gold-plating and colorizing. The statehood quarter series has been altered in these ways for sale to collectors. It is not illegal to alter a coin as long as the alteration is not done for deceptive purposes. Changing a mintmark, for example, from D to P because the P mintmark is more valuable for that coin would be against the law.

Historically, certain alterations are said to make specific U.S. coins luckier than they were before the alteration. Two examples of this are the love token and the hobo nickel. Although both alterations are still made today by altered coin artists, the heyday of love tokens was the latter half of the nineteenth century, and for hobo nickels, the Great Depression years of the 1930s.

Love Tokens

Love tokens are altered coins with an added message of love, luck, or friendship. Popular during the nineteenth and early twentieth centuries, they may be engraved with a name, with initials, or with a title or name, such as Mom. Artists who chose silver coins as their metallic canvas carved them. While all U.S. coin denominations were used, smaller coins were popular because they were inexpensive and dainty, like charms. Seated Liberty and Barber dimes were very popular among love token engravers.

Love tokens can be found all over the world, but silver American dimes and silver British sixpence likely account for most of them. Technically, these altered coins remain legal tender, but their value to collectors goes way beyond their face value.

To create a love token, the artist or jeweler first planed or buffed the reverse side of the coin until it was smooth. The obverse side of the coin containing the date was usually left unchanged, especially if the date had meaning for the intended recipient. Next, a pick or sharp tool was used to engrave initials or a brief message. A calligraphy-style or classic flowing script was a popular choice. Some type of decoration might be added, such as patterns or flowers. The final step was holing the coin or attaching a small loop to the top. In this way, the love token could be worn on a charm bracelet or as a pendant or pin. Some love tokens were created as Mother's Day gifts, but most were made or commissioned by people in love, to be given to their sweethearts.

Some examples of love tokens contain the legend "Good Luck" ringed by a horseshoe or decorated with other common lucky symbols. But even those without such sentiments are still considered lucky. Since time and affection were required to create love tokens, the end result was thought to bring all owners good fortune. When good fortune found the recipients of love tokens, they sometimes gave away their charms in order to share their good fortune with others.

Hobo Nickels

Hobo nickels first appeared as World War I began (the United States joined the fight in 1917), but they are most associated with the decade of the 1930s, when America suffered through the Great Depression. Fifteen million were jobless—about 25 percent of the workforce. Some homeless men took to "riding the rails," either to follow the agricultural work that had not been wiped out by drought or merely to have a roof over their heads and a few friends to talk to. To earn cash and pass the time, some of these so-called hobos started carving Buffalo nickels to sell or trade to people at railroad stations.

Since nickel is a very hard metal, this artwork took time and dedication. Unlike love tokens, where the old design is replaced, most hobo artists incorporated the Indian head or the buffalo into the artwork. Hobo nickels are still made, and some are carved on Jefferson nickels. Common designs include Santa Claus, soldiers, clowns, chiefs, and presidents. Buffalo are transformed into elephants and donkeys.

The luck in a hobo nickel was thought to be derived from the nickel itself and not the theme. Hobo nickels made unique lucky pocket pieces and are enthusiastically collected to this day. Many were given to children, thus igniting a lifelong interest in coin art.

Seven Sides

Seven is considered a very lucky number in several cultures, and it is a winning number in many well-known gambling pursuits. People may alter a coin's original round shape by giving it seven sides, with the intention of making it a lucky pocket piece.

Perhaps the most unusual altered American coin this author has ever seen is an 1836 seven-sided U.S. coronet large cent. Someone altered its original round shape many years ago to give it seven sides. U.S. large cent collectors shudder at the sight of an altered specimen (many have been holed for jewelry), and this change did lower the coin's estimated $16

Lucky altered coins: (left to right) a U.S. buffalo "hobo" nickel (1936; carved recently), a seven-sided U.S. large cent (1836), and a U.S. seated Liberty "love token" dime (1875).

large cent catalog value. Its value now lies in its appeal to the lucky coin collector. Given the right auction audience, it could sell in the same range or higher.

Seven-sided lucky coins are fun to collect. A surprising number of countries have issued them, especially in Europe. Some are minted with seven sides, and some are round with seven sides incused (i.e., stamped) around the edge.

The Hunley Civil War Good-Luck Love Token

The most famous single American lucky coin may be the 1860 double eagle from the *H. L. Hunley*, a submarine invented by the Confederates. When the *Hunley* was raised from the bottom of the ocean near South Carolina in August 2000, researchers found a bent and dented gold coin that had been a legend for more than a century. It was the Dixon love token.

Captain George E. Dixon received the large gold coin from his sweetheart, Queen "Queenie" Bennett, of Mobile, Alabama, when he joined the Confederate

Army. At the Battle of Shiloh, the coin in his pocket deflected a bullet and probably saved his life. Dixon had one side buffed smooth and engraved with three lines and his initials:

Shiloh
April 6, 1862
My Life Preserver
G.E.D.

Bennett's descendants found very similar engraving, an ornate cursive script that was probably created by the same person, in the back of her gold pocket watch. Her name was accompanied by the date December 25, 1862.

Queenie's watch contained a small photo, too, which is probably Dixon. The man in the photo is dark haired, handsome, and well groomed. His face wears a serious expression and a carefully manicured mustache. December 25, 1862, was the last Christmas Bennett and Dixon spent together. The following year, Dixon was in South Carolina working on the submarine project.

Seven-sided coins and round coins with seven sides incused are not uncommon: (clockwise from upper left) from Great Britain (1973), Spain (1987), Hungary "The Thinker" (dual date 1999–2000), Gibraltar 20 pence (2000).

Base-metal reproduction of the famous *Dixon-Hunley* gold coin love token. The original may be the most valuable lucky coin in the world.

Dixon carried his lucky pocket piece with him until February 1864, when he and the entire crew perished during a practice dive. This occurred only hours after the forty-foot *Hunley* went under the waves in Charleston Harbor to attack a Union blockade vessel, the two-hundred-foot USS *Housatonic*. The *Housatonic* sank, the first victim of a submarine attack in history, and Dixon's luck appears to have sunk with the Union ship.

The lucky gold coronet head $20 Dixon-Hunley coin resides at the Warren Lasch Conservation Center in Charleston, where the public can view it on weekends. Because of its fame and history, estimates of its value run into the millions of dollars. Fortunately, base-metal replicas of this historic coin are available for sale to the general public and to collectors.

Large Lucky Medals

Large lucky souvenir medals are an American phenomenon that began appearing in gift shops around 1914. Various commercial interests created large copper-plated and nickel-plated medallions two and a half to three inches in diameter, with lucky symbols and sentiments on one side and U.S. coin replicas on the other side. While there are examples of all de-

nominations (from penny to dollar) in existence, the vast majority of these heavy medals have an Indian head cent or Lincoln cent motif. The legend "Lucky Penny" usually frames the bust on the obverse. Dozens and dozens of varieties and modest prices make this a fun collectible. They also double as paperweights.

Large lucky souvenir medals wish the bearer good luck or "Health, Wealth and Happiness" and often feature common lucky symbols, like horseshoes, wishbones, elephants, and four-leaf clovers. The reverse side will also typically advertise an attraction such as Niagara Falls, a museum, a state fair, a national park, or an entire city or state. While these medallions are not nearly as common today in souvenir shops as they were throughout the twentieth century, they are still made and sold.

Two examples of three-inch diameter lucky souvenir medallions, both having an Indian head obverse with the legend "Lucky Penny." The first (undated) reverse reads, "Health, Wealth and Happiness," and the second (1960) features a Chicago museum.

Lucky Lindy Tokens

On May 21, 1927, Charles Lindbergh accomplished an amazing feat. He won a $25,000 prize for being the first person to fly alone and nonstop across the Atlantic Ocean from New York to Paris, and he did this in less than thirty-four hours.

The whole world followed the flight, gathering around radios for updates and cheering when the single-engine plane was spotted in French airspace. Ten thousand souls greeted him and his plane, the *Spirit of St. Louis*, upon landing. The press dubbed the aviator Lucky Lindy.

Almost immediately, medals and tokens commemorating the famous flight began to appear and were eagerly snapped up by people wanting to be as lucky as Lindy. By this time in U.S. history, many Americans were in the habit of carrying a "good-luck piece" (coin or token) in their pockets and purses. Some of these all-American brass and bronze pocket pieces were made in such great numbers that they are easy to find today, and surprisingly affordable, even in uncirculated condition.

Good-For Tokens

A good-for is a token that promises the bearer a service, an item of value, or a discount. The token is always "good for" something. Good-fors made in the early to mid-1900s often carried good-luck sentiments, too. One vintage example from a Minnesota hotel costs 50¢ but offers an "all you can eat" meal and "good luck," too. What a deal!

The famous lucky hula tokens of Honolulu, Hawaii, were once good for a bus ride, and their reputation as a lucky token is a free bonus. In 1951 the city of Honolulu created rapid transit tokens with pretty and slightly risqué hula dancers on both sides. Tourists immediately pocketed them for good luck and created a bus token shortage. The city was eventually forced to create a boring token without the dancers in order to stem the shortage. Happily, these pretty good-fors are inexpensive and readily available.

Also from Hawaii is the 1959 statehood one dollar trade token good for $1 in trade in the fiftieth state during its inaugural year. Also referred to as a *so-called dollar*, this silver-dollar-size gold-plated brass token is allegedly good for good fortune. The certificate that accompanied it declared the following:

> All coins have been blessed by a prominent Hawaiian kahuna (man of God), now deceased, in the hope that all who own one will enjoy good fortune.

Kadeco, of West Paterson, New Jersey, initially minted these trade tokens with a spelling error. The island of Oahu was misspelled as "Ohau." The error was corrected, but today the error "Ohau" tokens sell for a premium above the non-error "Oahu" version.

Sports and Gambling

Generally speaking, athletes and gamblers are a very superstitious lot. Both groups usually rely on some combination of skill and chance, and both tend to cherish lucky rituals. Baseball players, for example, have been known to wear lucky socks over and over again, presumably a pair they wore when they won an important game. Gamblers are big on lucky card decks and jewelry. Often, they will play at certain tables or slot machines because they feel luckier at those locations. And both athletes and gamblers use lucky coins and tokens.

The Super Bowl's Lucky Coin

Before every professional football game, a coin is tossed into the air after each team chooses heads or tails. The result of the toss determines who will kick off first and who will receive. The coin used at each annual Super Bowl, however, receives special attention. These coins, said to be very lucky, are sent to the National Football Hall of Fame after the game ends.

Sadly, there was no luck for a football player named Albert Glen "Turk" Edwards, a Rose Bowl star who in

A few All-American lucky tokens: (clockwise from upper left) Super Bowl XXXV "coin toss" coin replica (2001), Honolulu hula bus token (1951), Lucky Lindy token (1927), and Hawaiian trade dollar "Ohau" error token (1959).

Lucky casino coins include (clockwise from left) a ringed silver strike with Mr. O'Lucky from Fitzgeralds Casino in Reno, Nevada (undated), a $1 token from Fitzgeralds in Tunica, Mississippi (1994), and a $1 chip from Lucky Lola's in Cripple Creek, Colorado (undated).

Horseshoe-shaped encased Lincoln cent from the Horseshoe Hotel and Casino in Las Vegas, Nevada (1962), and "My Lucky Penny, Las Vegas" Lincoln cent elongate (1981).

1932 joined Boston's professional team, the Braves (renamed the Redskins in 1933). Edwards was a celebrity athlete in his time, official All-NFL in 1932, 1933, 1936, and 1937. An unlucky knee injury suffered at a pregame coin toss ended his career in 1940.

In recent years, the lucky coin toss has become more of an event. In 2000, for example, in a contest between Minnesota and Kansas, seven men from the Football Hall of Fame participated in the flip. These same individuals had played, coached, or managed in the other Vikings–Chiefs Super Bowl, Number IV, thirty years earlier.

Today's official Super Bowl flip coin, licensed by the NFL, portrays the Vince Lombardi trophy and the helmets of the two teams that are battling for the trophy. It measures one and a half inches in diameter. Private mints create a customized coin for the event, actually a medal, for it has no legal tender value, and then create duplicates of the lucky flip coin in silver and bronze for the collectors' market.

Casino Tokens
Casinos in Las Vegas, Atlantic City, and around the world have nothing to lose—and lots of business to gain—by encouraging the use of lucky tokens. Therefore, it is no surprise that many examples exist in this area. There are casino elongates, for one. These are regular pennies that have been smashed and rolled into thin ovals by special machines, to become "elongated cents." As the machine presses the coin, it engraves a new design and slogan, often wishing the bearer good luck.

Lucky casino pocket pieces also include casino encased cents, lucky pennies in aluminum holders on which are engraved lucky messages or symbols. And then there are casino chips, tokens, and silver strikes made of clay, plastic, bronze, silver ringed with bronze, or pure solid silver. All of these are readily available and highly collectible.

Lucky Advertising Tokens
In today's litigious atmosphere, no company would dare distribute advertising tokens that imply a prom-

ise of good luck lest they be sued by some unlucky soul for breach of contract. Modern lucky tokens feature symbols or characters, such as Fitzgeralds Casino's Mr. O'Lucky or Lucky Charms cereal's lucky leprechaun, but they promise nothing. They don't even offer a wish for good luck. Just a few decades ago, however, wishes, promises, and advertising good-luck pocket pieces were a common grouping. These fascinating tokens and medallions are numerous enough to easily and inexpensively enlarge a collection.

A few examples of lucky advertising tokens include encased cents from nightclubs, appliance companies, food products, and periodicals, such as the Kriss Kross tokens from the *Saturday Evening Post*. Even national parks advertised with lucky tokens made up for souvenirs. And there are so many examples from coin collecting clubs and shows that one could collect only these as a subspecialty and build a sizable collection.

A favorite in this category is from Bendix Automatic Washers. An aluminum-encased 1940s Lincoln cent is ringed with this legend:

> You can be as lucky as 2,000,000 Bendix owners; For distinguished service by the Bendix Automatic Washer, in 2,000,000 homes.

Wooden Nickels

Not all tokens are made of metal. Wooden money has been a popular American collectible since it was introduced in 1931 by a chamber of commerce in an isolated area of Washington state. A local bank had failed, there was a shortage of coinage, and flat square wooden "coins" were used as a temporary solution. By the mid-1930s, round wooden nickels, dimes, quarters, and dollars were being made for souvenirs, lucky pocket pieces, good-fors, and advertising devices. Coin clubs found them to be the perfect format to herald the coming of a coin show.

The old expression "Don't take any wooden nickels!" is used as farewell advice today in much the same way as the modern reminder to "Buckle up!" The warning derives from a specific type of wooden

Examples of advertising and good-for lucky tokens: (clockwise from upper left) Reading, Pennsylvania, Coin Club (1971); Ike Lucky Wooden Dollar (1971); All You Can Eat, Comstock Hotel, Minnesota; Bendix Automatic Washers encased Lincoln cent (1949); Grand Teton National Park (undated).

nickel, the good-for. Merchants working at town fairs and centennial celebrations were sometimes forced to stop accepting wooden nickels before their stated expiration date so that they would have enough time to redeem them. This left some customers holding on to nickels that no longer had any spending power.

In spite of the warning, many people do take wooden nickels because more than five million of them are still produced in the United States every year. They remain a fun tool for advertisers and an easy way to spread good luck—or at least good wishes—throughout a community.

The Franklin Mint and Lucky Token Advertising

The Franklin Mint of Pennsylvania was once the largest and most famous private mint in the world. Throughout the latter half of the 1960s and into the 1990s, the massive facility churned out millions of coins for many different countries, plus silver and bronze medals for collectors.

Between 1965 and 1969, the Franklin Mint created a series of medals for commercial interests, civic groups, and private individuals called SPIs, or special private issues. Each medal came packaged with a specifications card giving its mintage figures and metallic makeup. Several in the series were designed to be lucky pocket pieces with good-luck messages and lucky symbols. They were minted for Chevron Island, Heplon Incorporated, Midwestern United Life Insurance Company, and Minnesota Federal Savings.

Lucky Kids

Believing in things magical comes easier to children than it does to adults, so it should be no surprise that lucky pocket pieces have always been popular with kids. Savvy television show producers found a way to tie in these tokens with their children's programming. Children watching the Green Hornet, the Lone Ranger, Roy Rogers, and Hopalong Cassidy in theaters and on TV couldn't wait to be the first on the block with the matching lucky coin. Typically, the obverse featured the hero, usually a cowboy, and the reverse, a lucky horseshoe of some type. Generic versions of lucky cowboy tokens were made for the

tourist and restaurant trades. Some were also spinners, and others featured the Pledge of Allegiance on the reverse.

These pocket pieces were obtained a variety of ways. Cereal boxes and other food and goods marketed to children sometimes offered a free prize of a lucky coin. Lucky Charms cereal and Cracker Jack are two well-known examples. Kids could also write in to an address given after a television program. And toy stores used them as free giveaways.

During the 1940s and well into the 1960s, many American amusement parks and arcades had make-it-yourself lucky token machines that would create a customized aluminum token on the spot. These arcade-stamped tokens offered the buyer thirty-two spaces in which to stamp a message. Most blanks already had the legend "good luck" prestamped on the reverse.

Common messages included romantic sentiments and anniversary dates, but many parents also used

Four children's lucky pocket pieces: (clockwise from upper left) Hopalong Cassidy (undated), stamp-it-yourself arcade token (1950s), the Lone Ranger; reverse depicts Silver's Lucky Horseshoe (circa 1950), and Knotts Berry Farm, Buena Park, California (circa 1950).

these machines to create customized tokens recording the names and birth dates of each of their children. My father was among this group, and while he had no trouble finding machines for his first six children, by the time his seventh was born in the mid-1960s, he could no longer locate an arcade token machine.

Politics, Military, and War

A large and fertile field for the lucky numismatic collector is politics and the military. There is a diverse and interesting array of items to amass.

Because the 1930s was a time of widespread misfortune during the worldwide Great Depression, it is no coincidence that many American politicians called on good luck during their campaigns. Herbert Hoover (1874–1964), the thirty-first president of the United States, campaigned for his term that ran from 1929 to 1933 with a fascinating little token. With a Republican "lucky" elephant and the legend "Hoover Lucky Pocket Piece" on one side, the token offered its owner assurance by the message on the reverse: "Good for 4 Years of Prosperity." Within a few months of Hoover's taking the oath of office, however, the stock market crashed, and Americans lost their jobs in record numbers.

The companion to the Hoover lucky token is the Cooper lucky token. Myers Y. Cooper (1873–1958) ran as a Republican for governor of Ohio in 1928 and again in 1930 but was successful only the first time. His campaign token is a mirror copy of Hoover's except that "Hoover" is "Cooper," and only two years of prosperity is forecast instead of four. The Cooper token also specifies that the prosperity is good only "in Ohio." Presumably, if one carried this pocket piece out of state, prosperity stayed behind at the border.

As Hoover's single term wound down, Franklin Delano Roosevelt (1882–1945) began his first successful presidential campaign. A humorous token of his second term pictures him and his running mate, John Nance Garner (1868–1967), with the legend "Lucky Heads You Win Coin, 1936, Roosevelt, Garner," and a reverse that shows the backside of an elephant (symbolizing the Republican Party) lumbering into the

Lucky promises from political campaigns: (clockwise from upper left) Hoover (1929), "I Like Ike" encased cent (1956), Cooper (Ohio governor; 1930), and Franklin Delano Roosevelt (1936).

distance. Above the elephant, the legend is "Tails, You Lose."

General Dwight D. Eisenhower (1890–1969) became the thirty-fourth president of the United States in 1953. His campaign slogan, "I Like Ike," was short, sweet, and easy to remember. It translated well to a lucky pocket piece containing the slogan with a 1956 penny encased by an aluminum ring. The other side reads, "Keep Me And Never Go Broke." A four-leaf clover design finished the piece.

In Canada, a bespectacled Neil Cameron ran for political office in 1940 for the city of Toronto, Ontario. His token promised five years of good luck in exchange for a vote. The reverse reads, "I wish you good luck, 1940–1945," and depicts a handshake that is quite similar to the vintage Indian peace medals of the first U.S. presidents (and the 2004 Indian peace design U.S. nickel). The wrist of one hand is bare, and the other is covered with a cuff of cloth.

Even the United Nations jumped aboard the lucky bandwagon. The large UN aluminum token is undated but was probably made in the 1960s because it is a spinner. A spinner is a token made with a small bump in the center on which the token can be spun with a flick of the wrist. An arrow on the token points to the luckiest person present when the spinner stops spinning, or perhaps the person who would buy the next round of drinks. These peaked in popularity during the 1950s and 1960s.

This UN spinner points out the person who is sure to receive "Good Fortune." The wording on the reverse is "We the peoples of the United Nations pledge 'to practice tolerance and live together in peace with one another as good neighbors.'" This is followed by the arrow pointing to the edge with the legend "Good Fortune Follows Me." The UN building graces the obverse.

Military Challenge Coins
These lucky spinners proved to be as popular in the military as anywhere else and are the precursor of the widespread military challenge coin craze.

Today, many American military personnel carry a military challenge coin in one pocket. These are not technically coins but are large medals, about the size of a silver dollar. They are privately minted of bronze, are often colorfully enameled, usually contain the symbols and emblems of military services, and are created for several uses within the military. These uses include unofficial unit identification tokens, awards, commemoratives, lucky pocket pieces, and morale boosters. Their popularity has soared since the terrorist attacks of September 11, 2001, and now civilians are gobbling up these beautiful designs for their collections.

Military challenge coins take their name from the custom, dating back to the Korean War, of challenging a fellow soldier, sailor, or pilot in a nightclub to prove that the person was carrying at least one military challenge coin. If he or she could not produce it, the unlucky person lost the challenge and had to buy a round of drinks.

The Great War

Before anyone knew there would be a World War II, the First World War, of 1914 to 1918, was called the Great War. Many types of lucky tokens were minted by private companies during and after this worldwide conflict. Three of these varieties are described here.

The oldest is dated 1914 and features a lucky wishbone on the obverse. Made of bronze, it is a bit larger than a quarter. It reads, "Best wishes to you and yours." On the reverse is a thought-provoking verse:

> A Sentiment for 1914: Think big, talk little, love much, laugh easily, work hard, give freely, pay cash, be kind.

An undated U.S. Army token is next, made of brass, dating between 1916 and 1918. It shows three American soldiers in uniform marching with a flag. The legend takes no chances in that it invokes good luck and heavenly blessings. It reads

> United States Army
> God Bless America
> Good Luck to Our Army.

The final example is an advertising token from Brill Brothers "Ready To Wear" clothing. In addition to the name of the company and product, there is a large lucky horseshoe and a kind wish for the bearer:

> Victory 1918
> Your Country Thanks You
> May the Good Luck that brought you safely home be with you always.

Nonprofit and Religious

During the first half of the twentieth century, religious and other nonprofit organizations created tokens as fund-raisers, to increase awareness of their activities, and as souvenirs. Such organizations included orphanages, hospitals, schools, and medical research groups. Some of their tokens are fascinating and quite a few have luck themes.

Here are just a few examples of nonprofit lucky pocket pieces. A token dated 1924 from the Hospital for Joint Diseases asks the bearer to donate funds to complete construction. Calling itself a "Charity Luck Piece," it promises five blessings to generous donors. Next, a horseshoe-emblazoned bronze token wishes "good luck from our disabled" on one side and names its organization, Institute for the Crippled and Disabled, on the other side. Finally, an orphanage called the Hebrew Kindergarten and Infants Home, located at

35 Montgomery Street in New York City, circulated a "good-luck coin" with the irresistible legend "Have a heart, help the orphans, and God will help you."

In this category, you can also find lucky coins made by boys' and girls' clubs, civic organizations, and animal sanctuaries. One of these boys' clubs tokens advises, "Keep Me and Prosper." A popular collectible from the North Shore Animal League is an aluminum token with a dog side, "Dog Lover's Good Luck Charm," and a cat on the reverse, "Cat Lover's Good Luck Charm."

From left to right, World War I–era U.S. Army "Good Luck and God Bless" token (undated) and the Great War's "A Sentiment for 1914" token.

Unique, Strange, and Bizarre

Some lucky coins are just downright strange, even bizarre. These are great fun to discover and share. Often, people find it hard to believe that such odd tokens circulated widely in America.

For example, no alcoholic beverage company would promise you good luck nowadays for using their product. Instead, they carry warning labels for pregnant women. But the Green River Whiskey lucky token says, "It's lucky to drink" their product. Not to be outdone, the Clipper Ale lucky token offers a toast to "your good health" and for "success, health, wealth, love and romance."

Some examples are very limited about what they promise. A coin collector's medal dated 1965 specifically promises "numismatic luck" but only if "carried always." A fascinating good-luck coin from the American State Bank in Covington, Oklahoma, advises, "If you smile until 10:00 am, you will be happy the rest of the day."

"I bring Good Luck," brags an aluminum-encased Lincoln cent from 1930. This was minted during the dawn of the Great Depression, right after the stock market crash of October 1929. People really needed luck. This same era spawned the famous "Aint It Hell" lucky token. On one side, a grimacing face asks, "Aint it hell to be poor," and the reverse reads, "This entitles the bearer to $1,000,000 worth of

good luck." People down on their luck during the Depression liked the frank, honest tone of the token. The fact that no one with this token was ever enriched by a million dollars did not deter its adherents one bit.

Among those words one might associate with lucky, *Alcatraz* does not readily come to mind, and yet someone thought the two words made a fine pairing. The "lucky Alcatraz" coin bills itself as an "unusual gift from San Francisco." Created in 1974, this bronze medal comes with a card that offers a history of the famous island prison where some of America's most dangerous felons once lived.

The Billiken and the Gudlukk

The famous Billiken, the "god of luckiness and things the way they ought to be," was created and copyrighted in 1908 by Florence Pretz, a native of Kansas City, Missouri. She created a Buddha-like creature with a whimsical grin that was made into banks, tokens, and dolls.

Soon after, the Billiken traveled to Alaska, where it instantly became a good-luck symbol. Skilled Eskimo artists carved the little statue out of ivory for the

Bordering on the bizarre: (left to right) Numismatic Luck (1965), Alcatraz (1974), Aint It Hell (1930s).

tourist trade. Many kinds of Alaskan tokens and medals, including those made of silver, were struck with a Billiken on one side for good luck. Later, the Billiken became the mascot of St. Louis University in Missouri.

It is said that good luck and prosperity will come to those who rub the belly of the Billiken twice each day. The good-luck pocket piece reads

> I am the god of luckiness so always keep me nigh.

> Misfortune's frown will disappear at one flash from my eye.

> Be sure that I am on the spot when projects you begin.

> I am the god of luckiness. My name is Billiken.

A few years after the Billiken craze, the Rexall Drug Store chain developed a similar type of mascot and named it Gudlukk. They also took advantage of the popularity of civic clubs and organizations, such as the Improved Order of the Red Men (IORM), in creating a customer club. This Buddha-like little man wears a vest and a large horseshoe necklace around his neck. The Gudlukk token is a fun read:

> Optimistic and Progressive Order of Rexallites,
>
> Gudlukk, god of good luck, good health and good cheer,
>
> Member's coin.

The reverse contains this advertising:

> I am a Rexallite because my drug store needs, be they few or more, I can always buy best at the Rexall store. The Rexall store in my town is one of the world's best 7,000 drug stores.

The lucky swastika-like symbol on the reverse dates this piece to pre-Nazi times, probably the late 1920s. Because there were so many Rexall stores and because Gudlukk was popular with customers, many of these tokens were created. They are easy to find and fun to own.

The Swastika: From Lucky to Evil

If you collect lucky coins, sooner or later you will come across one with a "swastika" on it. The presence of the symbol of the Third Reich should not be construed as an endorsement of Nazi ideals. The truth is, the Nazi party borrowed this ancient symbol and ruined it forever. One small solace is that the swastika turned out to be anything but lucky for the short-lived regime.

The Navajo cross, also called the swastika, was a common symbol of good luck and prosperity on pottery and rugs of the Navajo, Pima, and Maricopa tribes of the southwestern United States until the 1940s. The ancient people of India, Tibet, and Turkey also used this design as a decoration.

The Navajo cross quickly lost its American Indian and lucky associations once the design was adopted by Adolf Hitler and used to represent the Nazi Party. The abrupt and total cessation of this common symbol on lucky coins of all types is a big help in determining when the undated examples were made: Lucky coins with the Navajo cross are pre–World War II (before 1939) and those without it, post–World War II (after 1945).

Multisymbol Lucky Tokens

Lucky clubs, which purport to generate good luck through club membership: (left to right) the Billiken (copyright 1908), Gudlukk's Order of the Rexallites (1920s), and the Worcester Salt Don't Worry Club (1930s).

Before World War II, when the swastika was still benign, multisymbol lucky tokens were very popular. A multisymbol token is one with many icons that purport to bestow good fortune on the owner. The idea here is the more the merrier. If one lucky symbol is good, several of them must be better. These tokens were said to concentrate the luck of all of the major lucky devices popular in American culture.

The 1934 Chicago World's Fair token is one example. The front of this bronze souvenir reads, "1934, A Century of Progress, Chicago." The reverse says, "Good Luck. 1833–1933. World's Fair." The design includes an elephant, a shamrock, a Navajo cross, and a horseshoe.

A famous token maker called Whitehead and Hoag created more than a few multisymbol lucky tokens. During the late nineteenth and early twentieth centuries, this Newark, New Jersey, company manufactured tokens and medals by the tens of thousands for social organizations, civic groups, clubs, nonprofit groups, politicians, and businesses. A collector could

spend a lifetime amassing tokens from this single company and never complete the collection.

The Whitehead and Hoag Mother's Day tokens are not difficult to locate, even after more than sixty years. They are often found holed because they were a popular jewelry item as well as a lucky pocket piece. The front of this brass medal depicts a woman sitting next to a vase of flowers with the simple legend "Mother." The reverse sports a shamrock, a wishbone, a Navajo cross, a horseshoe, and several other symbols. A little verse is centered:

> Every blessing, every cheer, every comfort, year by year;
>
> Every pleasure, glad dreams, too, is my wish for you, just you.

A Worcester Salt Company lucky token is another easy-to-find Whitehead and Hoag example. This company, which was later absorbed by the Morton

Pre–World War II multisymbol lucky pocket pieces: (left to right) World's Fair (1934) and Whitehead-Hoag Mother's Day medal (circa 1920–1930).

Salt Company, was situated in Warsaw, New York, a primary producer of salt for the country. This token is an advertising tool, a lucky pocket piece, and a club membership, all in one.

The front depicts the product (a bag of salt), the company name, and the motto "The Standard for Quality." The Worcester Salt token reverse is a collage of good-luck items: horseshoe, Navajo cross, wishbone, and shamrock. This wording rings the edge: "Membership emblem of the Don't Worry Club. Good Luck."

Lucky Paper Money
U.S. Banknotes

Paper money is not as old as coinage, and it needed time to catch on, but it is the dominant form of exchange in the world today. The oldest paper money is from China, dating back to the seventh century A.D. In the 1600s, Sweden was the first European nation to print banknotes.

Paper can be just as lucky as coins and tokens. In Singapore and Malaysia, for instance, married couples give single adults red packets of money for luck during the Lunar New Year. But in most cases, the luck in currency is found not in the color of the wrapper but in the serial numbers. Typically, serial numbers contain a short series of letters and a longer line of numbers. When one line runs its course, the numbers begin again with a new group of letters in front.

Consecutively numbered bills, kept together, are considered lucky. U.S. notes with ascending or descending order numbers (such as 1, 2, 3, 4, 5, 6, 7, 8 or 8, 7, 6, 5, 4, 3, 2, 1) are thought to be lucky. The luckiest serial numbers of all, however, are those with lots of 8s. The more 8s, the better. They are commonly called prosperity notes. The number 8 is considered to be extremely lucky among the Chinese for being a wealth builder, so Chinese-Americans often look for American paper money with one or more 8s to give as gifts. A bit less popular are banknotes with four or more consecutive 7s.

A few years ago, the U.S. Bureau of Engraving and Printing (BEP) tapped into this custom and sold specially packaged "lucky 8" dollar bills to the general public. Each uncirculated note has at least four 8s in a row in the serial number. They were a big hit. A red folder holds a note explaining the custom of "lucky money."

Other lucky serial number types include

Stutter numbers
Two numbers repeating, such as D59595959D.

Radar numbers
Sequences that are the same forward and backward, such as D34566543D.

Mismatched numbers
Top and bottom serial numbers that don't match—a rare and valuable error with U.S. money.

Single-digit numbers
Serial numbers made up entirely of a single digit. In 2004, for example, a 1969 Hong Kong $5 note in uncirculated condition sold for the astonishing price of $395 at an online auction. The reason? The numbers read, "222222."

Star notes
Also called replacement notes, because the star in the serial number indicates that this note replaced a defective one that was removed from the sequence at the printing facility. The U.S. error rate is low, roughly one in 100,000 notes. U.S. star notes will always sell above their face value in the collectors' market.

Money, Tokens, and Medals from Around the World
World Paper Money
Some nations have unique numbering systems, so it is best to consult a price guide before assuming that a serial number is rare. For example, a serial number beginning with the letters *AA* may not be the first ever printed. The first group may have been *A* or even *AB*. Star notes are not necessarily rare with some nations. In certain cases, a star is part of all serial numbers.

Chinese New Year Good-Luck Currency Sets
The Chinese believe in sharing good luck on New Year's Day. One way of doing this is to distribute

Enclosed is a $1 Note containing no less than
four number eights in a row (8888xxxx).
This note is considered a "Lucky Note" for many Chinese
because the number 8 means, "wealth, prosperity".
This note is an ideal gift for a family member
or friend that you want to extend
well wishes and the hope that they will
become wealthy and remain prosperous.

FEDERAL RESERVE NOTE
THE UNITED STATES OF AMERICA
THIS NOTE IS LEGAL TENDER
FOR ALL DEBTS, PUBLIC AND PRIVATE
B 88889949 M
WASHINGTON, D.C.
1

LUCKY MONEY

U.S. lucky paper money: prosperity note from the Bureau of Engraving and Printing (2000).

lucky coins and currency in red packets. To understand the makeup of these packets, you must understand the Chinese zodiac and its twelve animals, one of them a mythical creature.

The Chinese lunar calendar dates from at least 200 B.C. It is a twelve-year repeating cycle with each year in the cycle dominated by a different animal. Chinese culture holds that the animal ruling the year in which a person is born has a strong influence on personality. It is said, "This is the animal that resides in your heart."

There are two different legends about the origin of the zodiac. In the first, Buddha calls all of the animals to visit him before he leaves the earth. Only twelve show up, and he rewards them for this by naming a year in the calendar for each.

In the alternate legend, the twelve animals argue about who is to be first in the cycle of years. The gods settle the question by calling for a race from one side of the river to the other. All twelve animals gather at the river's bank and jump into the water. The rat hops up on the back of the ox and then jumps off and wins the race as the ox reaches the opposite shore. The animals finish in this order: rat, ox, tiger, rabbit, dragon, snake, horse, sheep, monkey, rooster, dog, and pig.

To determine your animal, find your birth year among these groups:

Chinese New Year good luck gift sets: paper money, coin, and medal for Year of the Ox, Rat, and Dog (1990s).

Animal	Birth Years
Rat	1924, 1936, 1948, 1960, 1972, 1984, 1996
Ox	1925, 1937, 1949, 1961, 1973, 1985, 1997
Tiger	1926, 1938, 1950, 1962, 1974, 1986, 1998
Rabbit	1927, 1939, 1951, 1963, 1975, 1987, 1999

Animal	Birth Years
Dragon	1928, 1940, 1952, 1964, 1976, 1988, 2000
Snake	1929, 1941, 1953, 1965, 1977, 1989, 2001
Horse	1930, 1942, 1954, 1966, 1978, 1990, 2002
Sheep	1931, 1943, 1955, 1967, 1979, 1991, 2003
Monkey	1932, 1944, 1956, 1968, 1980, 1992, 2004
Rooster	1933, 1945, 1957, 1969, 1981, 1993, 2005
Dog	1934, 1946, 1958, 1970, 1982, 1994, 2006
Pig	1935, 1947, 1959, 1971, 1983, 1995, 2007

For the last few years, private mints in China have released commercially prepared lucky New Year banknote and medal sets for sale all around the world. These typically contain a genuine small denomination banknote and aluminum coin of China, a medal of the current calendar animal, and bright red packaging in a red envelope because red is considered the luckiest color. These New Year sets are given as luck gifts.

In addition to the rat, ox, tiger, rabbit, dragon, snake, horse, sheep, monkey, rooster, dog, and pig, other animals and insects around the world have reputations as bearers of good fortune. These include the hen, eagle, ostrich, canary, turtle, frog, alligator, whale, dolphin, manatee, sea otter, carp, ladybug, cicada, cricket, cat, panda, bison, bear, bull, lion, elephant, rhinoceros, dinosaur, and (mythical) unicorn.

Million-Dollar Notes

There are two types of lucky currency that are not legal tender: million-dollar notes and hell notes. Million-dollar notes are designed to look very similar to U.S. dollars, Canadian dollars, and the paper money of other nations. The denomination printed on all four corners, however, is much higher than the average person ever sees.

There are companies that, for a price, will apply any portrait to the million-dollar note's center and add advertising copy to it as well. Coin and paper money dealers often have them printed up for advertising purposes and then distribute these lucky faux banknotes to potential customers.

The fact that the United States no longer prints large-denomination banknotes and has never issued a million-dollar note did not keep one woman from trying to spend one. Her attempt made the evening news in 2004 and resulted in her arrest when she tried to pass the fake bill in a department store.

Chinese lucky hell notes: the currency of the dead, who are awaiting reincarnation (undated).

Lucky Hell Notes

Hell notes are also called the *money of the dead* or *spirit money*. Part of a Buddhist tradition dating back thousands of years, they are decorated with lucky Chinese symbols. The word *hell* in this instance does not refer to the land of the damned but to a place where the dead reside while waiting to be reincarnated. Hell notes can be drab or very colorful and are highly collectible, but they are only legal tender on another plane of existence. The obverse usually features a depiction of the god of hell, the keeper of the gate and judge.

Every year during celebrations for the Chinese New Year, hell money is presented to the souls of ancestors who have passed on so that they can spend it in the afterlife. How is the money transferred? Western Union is of no help at all. The money changes hands by burning it to ash. The dead are also offered spending money soon after their funerals.

Lucky Sixpence—Backbone of a Worldwide Monetary System

In no way does the United States have a monopoly on lucky coins and related items. This type of numismatic item can be found on every populated continent. Expanding a lucky pocket piece collection outside American borders opens up a world of beauty and cultural diversity.

Some of our lucky coin traditions, including the lucky bridal sixpence, come from the United Kingdom. The humble sixpence (6p) is one of the British Commonwealth's oldest, best-known, and most beloved coin denominations.

Those of us who are not quick with sums, except multiples of five and ten, might assume that a monetary system based on the number six would be impossible to master, but the British have had centuries to grow accustomed to the unusual math. Consider these sextet-based denominations:

Coin	Value	Slang
Sixpence	6 pence	Tanner
Shilling	12 pence or two 6 pence	Bob
Florin	2 shillings	2 Bob
Half-Crown	2 shillings and 6 pence	Two and a Kick
Crown	5 shillings	5 Bob
Pound	240 pence or 20 shillings	Quid
Guinea	252 pence or 21 shillings or 1 pound plus one shilling	N/A

There were also several denominations below the sixpence:

Groat = 4 pence

Threepence = 3 pence or one-half sixpence (Slang is Joey–for silver issues)

Twopence = 2 pence

Penny = 1 penny

Half-penny = one-half of a penny

Farthing = one-fourth of a penny

The heart of the £.s.d. monetary system, where all coin denominations are divisible by the number 6, the 6p was first minted in the 1500s. The silver content was removed after 1946, the last one in a proof version was made in 1970, and it was demonetized in 1980. Yet this coin's popularity remains high. It is collected for its luck, beauty, history, and worldwide variety of design, as well as because of a little poem that promises to bring brides prosperity in their marriages. The poem tells us that every bride should have:

> Something old, something new,
> something borrowed, something blue,
> and a lucky sixpence in her shoe.

This rhyme has its roots in the early nineteenth century. The bride's coin is said to bring her wealth and happiness. To this day, brides all over the world slip a tanner (sixpence) into their left shoe before walking down the aisle.

Beginning in the sixteenth century, British sailors would sometimes bend a silver sixpence in one or two places before leaving port. The giver and sender would say, "From my love, to my love," when the bent coin was proffered. The sweethearts and wives would carry the lucky coins at all times. The bend in the coin reminded them not to spend the luck by accident.

In Colonial times, before the establishment of an official decimal-based currency, several U.S. states printed paper sixpence and briefly minted sixpence coins. In Victorian times, British sixpence were sanded and messages of love and affection were engraved on the little silver coins, including wishes for luck. And the luck was not restricted to Great Britain. The sixpence was once considered so lucky in the African Commonwealth nation of Zambia, for example, that many children were named Sixpence to help ensure their success.

Seven different British monarchs from the same "family tree": the lucky little sixpence was minted in Great Britain for four centuries and always with a monarch on the obverse. **Sixpence formats (left to right):** bent for love and luck, hand-engraved love token with initials *HA*, a silver Victorian sixpence, and one from 1948 that has been enameled. The sixpence on the bracelet is a Victorian "Young Head" sixpence. Dates range from early 1800s to 1948.

There was a time when "the sun never set on the British Empire" due to its global reach. As a result, many nations minted sixpence. Some of these are too scarce to be within the reach of the typical collector, but the good news is that most of the sixpence nations produced many coins. A total of seventeen have minted their own sixpence in good number, and while it is a challenge to collect them all in a type set, it is by no means impossible. A sixpence typeset would include one sixpence from every nation that ever minted a coin in this denomination. All of these are readily available for collectors, even those minted for just one year, and except for a few rare dates within a series, all are quite affordable. Most are the same size and weight as the British sixpence; a relative few are thicker, larger, or smaller.

The designs vary quite a bit, from birds and wild animals to flowers and stars. Most have the king or queen of England on the obverse, but some feature the elected leader of the country or a national symbol. The countries and dates of mintage are:

- Australia (1910 to 1963)
- British West Africa (1913 to 1952)
- Fiji (1934 to 1967)
- Gambia (1966)
- Ghana (1958)
- Ireland (1928 to 1968)
- Malawi (1964 and 1967)
- New Guinea (1935 and 1943)
- New Zealand (1933 to 1965)
- Nigeria (1959)
- Rhodesia (1964)
- Rhodesia and Nyasaland (1955 to 1963)
- Union of South Africa (1923 to 1960)
- South African Republic (1892 to 1897)
- Southern Rhodesia (1932 to 1952)
- United Kingdom (approximately four hundred years until 1970)
- Zambia (1964 and 1966)

Sixpence, Hobbits, and Hollywood

Lucky sixpence from Commonwealth nations (dates span the 1900s).

In times of coin shortages, British merchants made penny trade tokens in various denominations, including sixpence. You can also find miniaturized fantasy sixpence issues and sixpence game tokens. Even Hollywood makes a sixpence.

After the runaway success of the recent *Lord of the Rings* fantasy movies, one company minted lucky Hobbit sixpence in 2002 for sale to moviegoers and lucky coin collectors. The documentation accompanying these 90 percent silver fantasy issues claims that the sixpence is the most valuable unit of Hobbit currency.

These movie sixpence are "dated" 1402 and feature inscriptions in the Tengwar lettering and Kuduk language that author J.R.R. Tolkien invented to go along with his mythical world of Middle Earth. There is a fir tree on the obverse and the ancient Bridge of Stonebows on the reverse. The legend reads, "The Shire, abode of the Hobbits." (See illustration on page 76.)

Canada, France, Austria, Germany, and Ireland

Some Canadians claim that the national symbol, the maple leaf, is lucky. Certainly, it has a place of honor in the hearts of the people of Canada and on their penny, as well. Many of the same kinds of lucky pocket pieces common in the United States, from rolled pennies to encased cents, are found in uniquely Canadian versions. One 1970 encased cent reads, "Windsor Canadian Imported, The smoothest whiskey to ever come out of Canada."

The Canadian Lucky Loonie

At the 2002 Winter Olympics in Salt Lake City, Utah, luck took center stage–literally–when Trent Evans, an icemaker from Edmonton, Alberta, planted a Canadian dollar coin called a Loonie (for the loon bird) at the center of the hockey rink. He did this to mark the spot where the puck is dropped during the face-off. The coin was later covered with yellow paint so its presence was a secret. Was it simply coincidence that both the Canadian women's and men's hockey teams won gold medals on that very same ice? It had been fifty years since the last Canadian team won an Olympic gold medal in hockey.

The Canadians decided to celebrate the coin as well as the dual victory. At the Hockey Hall of Fame, the original Lucky Loonie is displayed in a special case that allows visitors to touch it. For the 2004 Summer Olympics in Athens, Greece, the Royal Canadian Mint created a special Lucky Loonie for the athletes to carry and for the Canadian public to enjoy. Above the loon bird is a maple leaf with Olympic flame design and the five Olympic rings. Some of these were specially packaged to raise money for the Olympic program. A special commemorative silver version (20,000 mintage) colorized at the mint was also created for the collector market. The rings are blue, orange, black, green, and red.

Lucky pennies and tokens (left to right): Germany (1925), Germany (1972), Canada (1970), and Canada (undated).

It's a good thing that Canada minted six million of the special Olympic lucky loonies because they have been traded and sold briskly since their appearance. Whether or not they bring luck may be debatable, but their immense popularity is certain. They may also have affected the standing of the Greek 2004 2-Euro bimetallic coin featuring a famous Olympic statue of a discus thrower. These circulation coins were a big hit among those attending the 2004 games and those watching them on TV around the world. They have become the new lucky pocket piece of the people of Greece.

Germany & Austria

Germans and Austrians love to exchange good-luck tokens, especially for the New Year. Encased lucky pfennigs (German pennies) are not uncommon in Germany. A 1972 copper New Year (Neu Jahr) token with a shamrock-sprinkled design wishes the bearer good luck. A fascinating advertising encased pfennig from 1925 recites a German adage: "Who the penny does not honor is not worth dollars." The aluminum ring includes a horseshoe and a shamrock.

Every year in Austria, a new lucky frog token is struck and distributed. The antics of the frog vary from year to year, but the message remains the same. Roughly translated, it is "Although I'm small and round, I'll bring you luck all year round."

Lucky Loonie (2004)

France

In France, the luckiest of coins is the French angel, which has been minted in various metals, including silver and gold, for more than a century. The French angel coin is surrounded with myths and legends of how it brought good fortune to its owners. It all started during the French Revolution, when the coin's designer, Augustine Dupre, the medalist to King Louis XVI, escaped the guillotine at the last moment due to a lightning storm. He is said to have given credit for his escape to the angel coin in his pocket. Legend has it that Napoleon Bonaparte carried an angel coin for good luck, too, but lost it right before he fought at Waterloo. Bad luck indeed.

Ireland

Some people claim that the luckiest coin in the whole world comes from a place that is itself considered lucky, Ireland. And that coin is the lucky Irish hen penny. When Ireland became a free state (independent of Great Britain) in the early twentieth century, the choice was made to keep the same monetary system: farthing, halfpenny, penny, threepence, sixpence, shilling, and so on. This coinage became obsolete at about the same time as Britain's sixpence because both nations went decimal in the late 1960s. But before the Irish penny shrank in size and changed its

Clockwise from left: the Austrian lucky frog copper token (2004), gold 20 francs good-luck French angel coin (1876), silver 10 francs good-luck French angel coin (1989).

The luckiest penny of all? Irish large hen pennies with the harp reverse were minted from 1928 to 1968. One has been holed for a keychain.

design, millions of hen pennies were made. Happily, this makes them affordable.

The large penny, or 1d (*d* stands for denarius), is a large bronze coin, about the size of a U.S. half-dollar. The obverse features the traditional Irish harp, and the reverse pays homage to the humble barnyard chicken surrounded by her chicks. The hen cent design was an immediate success, and collectors the world over happily added all of the Irish barnyard animal coins to their collections. These include the

Lucky cash coins: (clockwise from upper left) China (1821–50), Japan (1626–1844), Korea (1752), Vietnam (1802–19).

woodcock (bird) on the farthing, followed by the sow with piglets, hen and chicks, rabbit, Irish wolfhound (dog), bull, salmon, and horse.

You can find these large pennies made into various forms of lucky jewelry, too. Commercial enterprises and jewelry artists make them into pendants, money clips, and key rings.

China, Japan, Korea, and Laos

Ireland may be home to the luckiest penny, but China has claim to the title of nation with the greatest number and variety of lucky coins. Chinese culture is big on luck, and this is expressed in its coins, medals, paper money, tokens, and charms.

For more than two thousand years and up until the last century, the basic monetary unit of China was the humble "cash" coin. *Cash*, roughly translated, means "penny." Round on the outside and square on the inside, cash coins have a design that is said to represent heaven and earth, yin and yang, or masculine and feminine. These were made of various base metals, like copper and iron and bronze, and in such

"Charm"-ing but not legal tender: (clockwise from left) lucky cash-coin-type Chinese trigram replica (undated), silver fantasy Hobbit sixpence (minted in 2002 with the 'fantasy' date of 1402) amulet with a carousel horse (undated), and a Korean flower-shaped charm (undated).

numbers that even today, a cash coin made in Christ's lifetime can be bought for less than $10.

Cash coins come in an amazing array of sizes, denominations, and metallic alloys. Almost every Asian nation has minted them at one point. Their beautiful ancient patinas make them an intriguing collectible. And, of course, they are said to be very lucky. Feng shui enthusiasts recommend hanging a cash coin from the ceiling of a home with red thread to bring good luck inside. *Feng shui*, literally "wind and water,"

Antique lucky dragon coins of Asia: (left to right) China, Hu-Poo 20 cash (1917), and Japan, 2 sen (1890s).

Modern lucky dragon coins of Asia: (left to right) North Korea, 1 won blue dragon (2000), and Taiwan, 10 yuan (2000).

is a set of ancient principles for planning and arranging inside décor.

Collectors will also enjoy amassing ancient lucky Asian cash-shaped charms and modern reproductions. Also called amulets, these are similar to cash coins but were never legal tender. Charms are said to chase away evil and attract good luck. They have designs such as animals, instead of simply letters (Chinese characters). Some are minted as amulets and some are hand-carved from genuine cash coins, not unlike U.S. love tokens.

One type of lucky charm is larger than a silver dollar and has eight sets of three bars all the way around it in a circle; they ring the reverse. These trigrams represent natural forces, such as fire, water, thunder, and earth, a design that is more than two thousand years old. The benevolent expression on the charms translate as, "Let the wealth grow and treasure come in the house." The charm is said to activate the "essence of good fortune" and bring happiness to the members of the household in which it resides.

Lucky silver and gold fish coins: (left to right) Laos, silver 15,000 kip, mint-colorized flower horn fish (2003–04), and China, gold 5 yuan, boy with carp (1997).

Korean charms are smaller, half-dollar size, and some have a flower-shaped edging. The example in the following illustration has an eight-sided hole in the center and eight petals around the edge because 8 is a lucky number in Korean culture. The characters on some Korean charms translate roughly as "coins used through highs and lows, rich and poor." Some have Chinese zodiac animals; most contain some sort of wish for prosperity.

While these charms are fun to collect, beware of spending too much for them. Counterfeit "antique" charms are everywhere, and sometimes only an expert can tell the genuine from the artificially aged phony. Therefore, it is safer to assume that the charm is a modern reproduction and pay accordingly.

The dragon is a mythical creature found in cultures from the Middle East to Europe and Asia. In Christian cultures, the dragon is associated with evil. On coins, the dragon is usually facing the spear point of St. George. In Asian cultures, however, the dragon is good and strongly associated with good luck, fortune, and the New Year.

The dragon coins of Asia span many decades, come in different sizes and denominations, and constitute a fascinating area of lucky coin collecting. And there are many modern issues, too, including quite a few issued by nations on other continents. Dragons and Y2K have something in common. Since many nations minted several new designs in 2000, a millennium coin collection can be surprisingly substantial. And the dragon was a favorite subject because the year 2000 is also the Year of the Dragon on the Chinese calendar.

The boy with carp design has been portrayed on various Chinese coins and medals for many years. Shou Cai Tong Zi, the boy who guards fortune in a traditional Chinese legend, is shown holding a large fish, the ancient symbol of continuing abundance. One example is a commemorative gold coin of China, legal tender in the People's Republic of China, with a 5 yuan face value and containing 1/20 ounce of pure gold.

Another lucky fish coin, this one from Laos, received the Most Popular Coin Award at the Asia Money Fair when it debuted in 2003. The Laotian flower horn fish coin comes in several sizes and denominations. Pictured is the 15,000 kip colorized silver version with a latent image date that changes from 2003 to 2004 when the coin is turned slightly.

The black spots on this humpbacked fish resemble Chinese characters. It is believed that the bigger the hump on any of these tropical fish, the more luck there will be for the owner of the fish. The writing on the coin makes a reference to abundance, a wish for the buyer.

There are numerous private mints within and outside of China that make and market lucky numismatic collectibles to people around the world. The beautiful Chinese Lucky Bat Vault Protector is one example. Its formal name is the Gold Coin of the Five Blessings and Auspicious Clouds, even though it is a medal.

Combining elements of Chinese myth and legend into one small 1/10th ounce of gold, this popular issue purports to protect a coin collection from theft and catastrophe. It is made in a traditional cash coin design with a square hole in the center. A circle of bats on the reverse create a powerful air of luck and protection. The wording says the coin is designed to "induce fortune and treasure" and the "fulfillment of every wish in mind." It is packaged in an individually numbered red folder for lucky New Year gift giving. Five thousand of this version from 1990 were minted.

Liberia

Elephants have been considered symbols of good luck in many countries for centuries. Several countries have put the lucky elephant on their coins at one time or another, but Liberia is one that has done so consistently. For almost fifty years beginning in 1937, Liberia paid homage to the elephant on its minor coins—that is, half cent, cent, two cents, and five cents. And today, the elephant is featured on commemorative coinage. These lucky Liberian elephant coins are highly prized by collectors and are easy to find.

In 2000 the Republic of Liberia celebrated the lucky Chinese zodiac by minting a set of twelve shiny copper-nickel $5 coins, one for each animal. These are very pretty and surprisingly inexpensive. In that same year, Liberia also took the term *lucky coin* to a whole new level with the issuance of a silver $10 coin called the "world's luckiest coin." Colorized by the American Historic Society, this coin is designed to concentrate luck for its owner by depicting a large group of traditionally lucky symbols on the reverse. These include the elephant (of course), a shamrock, a ladybug, a lucky number 7, a shooting star, a horseshoe, and the *hamsa* hand. Within the Jewish tradition, the *hamsa* is a symbol of good fortune, blessings, and protection.

Commercial Lucky Coin and Medal Collections: Many Nations

In 1976 the Franklin Mint created and sold a set of beautiful medals in both silver and bronze with lucky themes from cultures and nations around the world. The set was accompanied by twelve folders describing the symbolism behind the chosen icons, as well as the history of the designs. The reverse of each medal has a legend that identifies the symbol depicted and its place of origin, plus the legend "Good Luck" in the appropriate language. These interesting sets can be found occasionally for sale at online auctions in coin, bullion, and medal areas.

Five lucky bats! China, cash-coin-look-alike gold medal, Gold Coin of the Five Blessings, in red folder (1990).

The dozen medals represent these lucky themes:

1. Assyrian scarab

2. Japanese Hotei

3. Roman cornucopia

4. Egyptian cat

5. Irish four-leaf clover

6. Indian elephant

7. Persian simurgh

Franklin Mint lucky medals of the world sample obverses: Indian elephant and Chinese dragon (all 1976).

8. Greek fish

9. Amish hex sign

10. English cricket

11. Hebrew Chai

12. Chinese dragon

Lucky coins are native to virtually every coin-producing culture on the planet. Therefore, it was only a matter of time before a private mint or commercial enterprise decided to package a group of lucky coins from around the world.

The American Historic Society is responsible for a group collection called simply Lucky Coins (product number AHS-4850). It consists of a lot of twenty-five uncirculated small coins from twenty-four different countries (two types are from Italy), each with a lucky symbol, word, or phrase. The dates span the 1980s and 1990s.

The short information sheet says just enough about each coin to whet the reader's appetite for more knowledge. For example, one of the Italian coins has a dolphin on one side. These friendly sea mammals are considered lucky by many different cultures because species of dolphins are found all over the world. There are many legends of dolphins helping to save drowning humans. Dolphins were one of the first animals ever to be placed on a coin, in ancient times, and they remain a popular coinage theme to this day.

This world lucky coin collection is no longer made by the American Historic Society, but these sets can be found with some regularity in coin shops and at on-

Franklin Mint silver lucky medals of the world: (top row, left to right) Assyrian scarab, Japanese Hotei, and Roman cornucopia.
Franklin Mint lucky medals of the world: (left to right) Egyptian cat, Irish four-leaf clover, and Indian elephant.
Franklin Mint lucky medals of the world: (left to right) Persian simurgh, Greek fish, and Amish hex sign.
Franklin Mint lucky medals of the world: (left to right) English cricket, Hebrew Chai, and Chinese dragon (all 1976).

line auction venues. With a little patience, you can add this intriguing group to your collection.

The AHS Lucky Coins collection consists of the following:

1. Andorra, new 1 centime, Cornucopia
2. Bermuda, 1 cent, Prosperous Pig
3. Botswana, 5 thebes, Lucky Toko Bird
4. Brazil, 10 cents, Panning for Gold
5. Cook Islands, new 5 cents, the famous Fertility God Statue
6. Cyprus, 2 cents, Minoan Bulls
7. Eritrea, 10 cents, Ostrich with Lucky Feathers
8. Ethiopia, 1 cent, Lucky Lion
9. Hungary, 50 forint, Bridge to Prosperity
10. Iceland, 10 aurar, Bull of Good Fortune
11. India, 25 paisa, Rhino with Horn (Fertility)
12. Ireland, 1 penny, Lucky Irish Penny
13. Italy, 5 lira, Lucky Dolphin
14. Italy, 10 lira, Green, Lucky Color
15. Jamaica, 1 cent, Food for Long Life
16. Lithuania, 5 cents, Angels and Heart
17. Malaysia, 1 cent, Sacred Drum
18. Peru, 5 cents, Lucky Inca Symbol
19. Russia, 1 kopek, St. George Slaying the Unlucky Dragon
20. South Korea, 5 won, Turtle Boat (turtles represent long life)
21. Swaziland, 5 cents, Lily (Symbol of good fortune)
22. Tanzania, 50 cents, Rabbit
23. Turkey, new 50,000 lira, High Value Makes You Rich
24. Zambia, 25 ngwee, Crowned Horn Bill (a royal bird)
25. Zimbabwe, 25 cents, Rabbit

American Historic Society Lucky Coins of the World: part I (from 1980s and 1990s).
American Historic Society Lucky Coins of the World: part II (from 1980s and 1990s).

The Most Famous Coin Collection in History

Even though you don't have to be rich to collect lucky coins, there is one collector who personifies the reference to coin collecting as the "hobby of kings." One of the most famous and valuable coin collections ever amassed belonged to King Farouk of Egypt (1920–65; ruled 1936–52). His collection contained more than 8,500 coins and medals, from all over the world, including the coin that holds the record for highest auction price. The rare 1933 U.S. double eagle

gold that he once owned sold for $7.59 million in 2002.

King Farouk was famous and disliked for his excessively lavish lifestyle and for his kleptomania. He enjoyed pilfering items on state visits and once stole a pocket watch from Winston Churchill. He was nicknamed the Thief of Cairo. The king kept a large staff busy buying coins for his massive collection, but he was somewhat indiscriminate. He bought the rarest of the rare as well as much more ordinary uncirculated coinage, too.

When the ultimately unlucky monarch was deposed and

King Farouk of Egypt, a prodigious coin collector and subject of legal tender coins, too: silver 5 piastre (1939).

exiled to Europe in 1952, the Egyptian government sold his collection. The huge auction in 1954 was called the greatest numismatic event of the twentieth century. To this day, even common coins that have a Farouk collection "pedigree" sell for a premium.

For collectors who cannot afford a coin from this collection, the next best thing may be an Egyptian coin with Farouk's bust. These Egyptian legal tender coins, depicting the most famous coin collector in history on a legal tender coin, were issued in the 1930s in various denominations and in such numbers that their prices remain modest to this day. ◼

4

THE INSTANT EXPERT QUIZ

Diligence is the mother of good luck.
                              —*Benjamin Franklin*

1. Name three reasons why people collect coins.

2. List two lucky words or phrases associated with the culture of Ireland.

3. Has any scientific study to date found that lucky pennies produce luck?

4. What is the difference between a coin, a token, and a medal?

5. For a penny to be "lucky," must it be found heads up or tails up?

6. Define *exonumia*.

7. What are the most important tools a coin collector needs?

8. To detect a counterfeit coin, what should you measure?

9. What is a love token?

10. What is a military challenge coin?

11. The Billiken mildly resembles which religious figure?

12. A swastika on a lucky coin suggests what about its date of manufacture?

13. Who is meant to spend hell notes?

14. What should a bride put in her left shoe for good luck?

15. Which animal brings good luck to Austrians?

16. Which barnyard animal can be found on the Irish lucky penny?

17. List two of the four major online resources for buying lucky coins, tokens, medals, and collecting supplies.

18. Why should you never purchase anything online if you are not using updated antivirus, firewall, and security software?

19. Name three of the six major offline coin buying resources.

20. List two ways that a rare coin can enter circulation.

Answers

1. People collect coins for many reasons, including fun, nostalgia, challenge, investment, a love of history and art, to learn more about other cultures, and to be able to act as a curator for their own small metallic museums.

2. Irish terms or phrases that are associated with good luck include *shamrock*, *four-leaf clover*, *leprechaun*, *pot o' gold*, *shillelagh*, *Blarney stone*, *claddagh*, *St. Patrick's Day*, *wearin' o' the green*, and *lucky charms*.

3. No, but the people carrying them often feel more confident and optimistic, which can have a positive effect on their lives.

4. A coin can only be called a coin if it is or was legal tender. Tokens are coinlike in that they can sometimes be used like a coin. Medals commemorate something or someone.

5. Heads up.

6. *Exonumia* refers to those items of numismatic value that are not coins, such as tokens and medals. It means literally "outside of coins."

7. Good lighting, a magnifying glass, coin storage and cleaning supplies, and a price guide.

8. Check the proper weight, size, and thickness of the item against the specifications listed in your price guide.

9. Love tokens are altered coins with an added message of luck, love, friendship, or something as simple as a pair of initials.

10. These are not technically coins, but large medals, about the size of a silver dollar. They are privately minted of bronze and often colorfully enameled, usually contain the symbols and emblems of military services, and are created for several uses within the military. These uses include unofficial unit identification tokens, awards, commemoratives, lucky pocket pieces, and morale boosters.

11. Buddha.

12. That it was made before World War II, before the swastika was a Nazi symbol.

13. The dead who are awaiting reincarnation.

14. A sixpence.

15. The frog.

16. Hen and chicks.

17. There are four major online resources for buying lucky coins, tokens, medals and collecting supplies via computer: major online auction venues, retail Web sites or cyberspace stores, e-mail coin listings, and buying directly from major world mints and medal makers.

18. There are viruses that can infect your hard drive and relay sensitive information to crooks around the world.

19. There are six major offline resources for buying lucky coins, tokens, and medals: mail order through

magazines and mint sales, coin shops, coin shows and conventions, coin clubs, estate sales and auctions, and flea markets and yard sales.

20. A rare coin may enter circulation through heirs who do not know about the coin's value or thieves who steal a coin collection and don't realize what they have. ◼

RESOURCE GUIDE

Some luck lies in not getting what you thought you wanted but getting what you have, which once you have got it you may be smart enough to see is what you would have wanted had you known.

—Garrison Keillor

Collecting lucky coins is like taking a cross-country vacation by train—getting there is half the fun. Reaching your collecting goal is nice, but the searching and buying are just as satisfying for many people. The keys are to know what you want and what you can afford to spend and to identify the best opportunity to purchase at the lowest price.

For example, if you are looking for a Franklin Mint lucky medals set in proof bronze at an online auction site, you may wish to type in the search term every few days to see what's available. You may see one set with a starting bid of $120. But if you wait and keep looking, you might find a set with a starting bid of $1 or a buy-it-now price of $90. In other words, you don't have to jump at every opportunity. Patience can save you lots of money in the long run.

RESOURCES FOR BUYING AND SELLING

Nowadays, there are three ways to buy: online (with a computer), offline (without a computer), and a combination of both. Each of the first two types has its own distinct advantages and disadvantages. Buying online is fast, easy, convenient, and, if you are a fan of auctions, exciting. The competition also tends to keep prices down. But unlike offline venues, you can't see, touch, or examine the items up close before you buy. Offline resources are more personable and less stressful. Dealing directly with people gives you an opportunity to learn more about the items you are buying. You and the seller get to develop a relationship, perhaps one that will last for many years.

The person who shops locally and with a computer has the best of both worlds. This collector can choose the shopping method best suited to the item or items required.

Online Buying

For the online buyer, there are four major online resources for lucky coins, tokens, medals, and collecting supplies:

major online auction venues

retail Web sites or cyberspace stores

e-mail coin listings

Web sites of major world mints and medal makers

Addresses on the World Wide Web

Addresses on the Web tend to change much more frequently than physical addresses. Electronic merchants merge, domain names are bought and sold, and businesses change Internet service providers or Web hosts. Often, the old link will send you to the new link. In other cases, you will need to use a search engine to find the new URL.

The best way to locate the latest URL is to use a search engine. Search engines are the online version of a library card catalog. They are the address books of the Internet. There are many search engines to choose from—for example, Yahoo!, Google, Ask Jeeves, Kanoodle, LookSmart, MSN, and Open Directory—so if the first one does not help, try another. You can get search results from a large number of search engines at *www.search.com*.

Major Online Auction Venues

There are two kinds of auction Web sites: those that deal mostly with minor coins and less valuable collections with a few valuable coins and those that sell almost exclusively certified or high-end coins, medals, and collections. Unless you are an expert, consider the first group first and minimize your financial risk while you learn. When you are ready to buy the scarcer lucky coins, check out the high-end Web sites.

The following lists are not exhaustive. They are designed to give buyers an overall picture of what's available.

Mostly Common to Midrange Coins and Exonumia
Amazon.com Auctions, http://s1.amazon.com.
eBay, www.ebay.com.
uBid, www.ubid.com.
World Exonumia, www.exonumia.com.
Yahoo! Auctions, http://auctions.yahoo.com.

Mostly Certified and High-End Coins and Medals
Heritage Galleries and Auctioneers: Rare Coins and
    Currency, www.heritagecoin.com.
Teletrade Auctions, www.teletrade.com.
Bowers and Merena Auctions,
    www.bowersandmerena.com.
Certified Coin Exchange, www.certifiedcoinexchange.com.

Online Auction Bidding Strategies

Three of the largest and most popular computer coin auction companies are eBay, Amazon, and Yahoo! Auctions. It is probably safest to master the art of online bidding at one of these sites because they have excellent guides for beginners. Once you have experience, you can bid intelligently at other auction Web sites.

There are definite steps you can take to get the best items possible for the least amount of money. As a buyer, you should do the following:

1. Read the auction description carefully, including the forms of payment accepted (check, money order, etc.) and the shipping cost (which can vary widely from seller to seller).

2. Next, check the seller feedback or rating to see what previous customers thought of the seller's products, service, and packaging. If you see more than a few negative comments or some that are recent (within the last three months), think twice.

3. Third, save this auction to your "watch list" while you look for similar items and comparison shop. Check the search box for similar items that might be in better condition or offered for a lower starting bid or "instant buy" price. Also check the "completed

auctions" search for similar items that have sold recently and what their final bid amounts were.

4. Finally, if you have a price guide, look up the item or items in the price guide to see how the current bid compares.

5. If after taking all of these steps you are satisfied that this is a good deal from a reliable seller, place your bid.

6. Lots of early "bidding wars" only serve to raise the final price. Try to bid later in the auction.

7. You can bid your maximum and allow the software to increase your bid as needed up to that maximum, or you can "swoop" (or "snipe"). To swoop, place a bid in the final seconds; twice the current bid is generally a safe range. If someone else has already bid a higher maximum, however, your swoop will fail. To avoid disappointment on an item you really want, always bid your true maximum.

Other Tips

In addition to researching an item and bidding with patience, the successful auction buyer looks out the window once in a while. In very cold weather, more people are paying attention to their inside hobbies—like buying coins, medals, and tokens. The evening hours or prime-time and weekend evenings are also popular bidding times, when competition is at its greatest. If you can find coin auctions ending during business hours, in hot weather, or very late at night, you are likely to have less live bidding competition. Unless a reserve price has been placed on the item, less bidding competition means a lower final price.

Retail Web Sites or Cyberspace Stores

Here are some suggestions of where to purchase coins, tokens, and collecting supplies.

- **American Coin and Stamp Brokerage,**
  www.acsb.com.
  A brokerage dealing with coins, rare coins, U.S. coins, and coin collecting supplies.
- **Brooklyn Gallery of Coins and Stamps,**
  www.brooklyngallery.com/shopping/shopping.htm.

A gallery specializing in supplies and accessories for the coin collector, including albums, books, holders, folders, and mounts.

· **Japanese Style Inc.,** www.japaneseweddingfavors.com/chinese_red_envelopes.asp.
A Minnesota retailer selling red envelopes, Chinese red envelopes, lucky coins, lucky Chinese coins, I Ching coins for wedding favors, and Chinese New Year and Chinese party favors.

E-Mail Coin Listings

These Web sites allow you to sign up for e-mail coin lists or catalogs from which you can choose items to purchase. They are also happy to accept your wish list. These coin lists also contain interesting articles and background information on the coins and tokens.

Chuck D'Ambra Coins, http://telesphere.com/index.html.
Coin Lode, www.coinlode.com/index.htm.
Dealer of animal coins.
Joel's Coins, www.joelscoins.com.
Washington Square Coin Exchange, www.wscoin.com.

Buying Directly from World Mints and Medal Makers

Buying direct can save money because an item that sells out quickly will cost much more in the secondary marketplace. Mints will also send out emails about special items and sales.

Government Mints and Large Distributors

The British Royal Mint, www.royalmint.com.
Euro Collections International, www.eurocollections.com.
A retail distributor of new European, Asian, and African coins from various mints.
The Mexican Mint (*La Casa de Moneda de México*), www.cmonedam.com.mx/cmm/cmm_bastidores_i.htm.
PandaAmerica, www.pandaamerica.com/index7.asp.
A retail distributor of new coins from many world mints, especially Asian countries.
Pobjoy Mint, www.pobjoy.com/pobjoy.asp.
A manufacturer of coins for many nations.
The Royal Australian Mint, www.ramint.gov.au.
The Royal Canadian Mint, www.rcmint.ca.
The United States Mint, www.usmint.gov.

Private Mints

Alaska Mint, www.akmint.com.
A manufacturer of nuggets, medals, tokens, coins, medallions, and coin jewelry.

American Commemorative Mint, www.amcomint.com.
A manufacturer of medallions geared toward commemorating those who serve in the four major branches of the armed forces.

American Historic Society (AHS), www.ahs.com.
A distributor of U.S. coin groupings, specialized medals, coins (including altered and colorized coins), tokens, and coin jewelry.

American Mint, www.americanmint.com.
A distributor of commemoratives and collectibles, specializing in commemorative medals of America's history.

Modern-Day Treasure Hunts

A fun and potentially profitable numismatic auction to look for is the online estate sale. Sometimes, heirs will auction a box of tokens that Grandma had saved or an album of coins from a parent. If the scans or photos are not clear, contact the seller by e-mail before the auction ends and ask for more scans or for a sampling of information. Your e-mail could read this way:

> Dear Seller:
>
> I am interested in bidding on your auction #12345678, the box of coins and tokens, but the scans are not clear enough on my computer screen for me to make out any detail. Do you have any close-up shots you could send me via e-mail? If not, would you please pull three to five coins and tokens at random and tell me the wording and dates on both sides? In this way, I can get an idea of what is included. Thank you.

Bidding carefully on these inheritance collections will produce many more happy moments than disappointments. In one case, a medal at the very bottom of an estate box looked interesting and was in immaculate condition. The buyer sent it to a professional authentication service that advertised in her coin magazine. The response indicated that this was an uncirculated French jeton medal and was almost two hundred years old. It was valued at $200.

In another case, a buyer found a thin, dime-sized, ancient-looking coin with Arabic-type writing on it. It was dirty and ranged in color from light brown to black. The coin was stapled inside of a yellowed cardboard 2x2 with a single question mark written on one corner.

The buyer set the ugly little coin aside, planning to research it some other time. A year later, it was rediscovered in inventory while the owner was preparing a lot of duplicates for sale. He almost added it to the group, but something about it made him curious.

It took a while (since he doesn't read Arabic) to research price guides for the mystery coin's correct nation of origin (Turkey) and century (eighteenth). As he matched its size to one in a group of similar-looking coins, it appeared to correlate perfectly to a gold coin pictured in the huge catalog. He placed it into a glass bowl and poured in a bit of solution designed to safely clean gold coins. As he swished the solution around, the coin gradually began to change color. Gold was shining through the grime. Within thirty seconds, it was a beautiful light yellow! It was indeed a gold coin and valued at more than $150. Talk about feeling lucky!

Of course, not all estate sale collections will yield such serendipitous items. And sometimes, a seller will list a box of common duplicates as a "rare estate sale find," so caution is called for. Decide how much you want to risk in advance. In this way, you won't feel cheated if the collection is ordinary.

A Word About Security
Never purchase anything online if you are not using updated antivirus, firewall, and security software. There are computer viruses (malicious software code) that can infect your hard drive and relay sensitive information to crooks around the world. And these viruses grow more sophisticated every day. This is why it is crucial to keep your security software

current. The best programs automatically download their own updates on a regular and frequent basis.

Since criminals buy up abandoned domain names and create more with names spelled very much like legitimate businesses, it is imperative to check out Web sites very carefully. Never give your credit card information to any business, even one of those listed here, unless you have checked it out first. Ask other collectors about their experiences, check out the Better Business Bureau Web site, and listen to your own intuition. If a Web offer (or any offer) sounds too good to be true, it probably is.

There are services you can use that will protect your financial information. PayPal (www.paypal.com) allows you to use a credit card or your checking account to pay almost anyone, but only PayPal sees your account number and expiration date. Western Union (www.westernunion.com) will (for a fee) send a money order for you anywhere in the world, and you can pay for it with a credit or debit card.

Once you are registered at auction and payment Web sites, beware of spoofs. A spoof e-mail is one designed to look legitimate but is not. Criminals with the intent of stealing your identity or your money send spoofs. For example, you may receive a spoof from someone claiming to work for PayPal Security. It may even have a PayPal look to it. But if the e-mail is asking you to reveal passwords or sensitive personal or financial information for any reason, be suspicious. Forward the spoof to PayPal, and then delete it. Never respond to these messages. Legitimate businesses will never ask you for such information.

Finally, never give out your street address for any reason, even if your collection's value is humble or you keep your collection in a safety deposit box at the bank. You don't want someone to sell your address to a thief. It doesn't cost much to rent a small post office box. They can start at around $25 per year. If you need a physical address for non-USPS deliveries, use your work address or some other commercial address. You can also rent a box with a physical address from companies like the UPS Store.

Offline Buying

For people who prefer not to use a computer for buying, there are six major offline resources for buying lucky coins, tokens, and medals:

- mail order through magazines and mint sales
- coin shops
- coin shows and conventions
- coin clubs
- estate sales and auctions
- flea markets and yard sales

If you are fortunate enough to live near one of the branch mints in Denver, Philadelphia, or San Francisco, you will enjoy browsing and buying in the gift shops. There was a time several generations ago when coin collectors who needed to fill a slot in a U.S. collection simply wrote to the U.S. Mint requesting to buy the needed coin. If you wanted a certain series of bronze medals made over in silver, you could order them from the U.S. Mint, provided you were able to supply the silver bullion. Times have changed, however. The U.S. Mint still sells coins and medals but only those minted recently, and they no longer fill custom orders.

MAIL ORDER, SHOPS, AND SHOWS

Today's offline buyer can visit the local coin shop; attend club meetings, shows, and conventions; stroll through yard sales; or order through magazines. All of these options remain popular, although there are far fewer coin clubs than in decades past. Some people attribute this to the extreme time constraints of today's lifestyle, but others say that club membership is simply moving into cyberspace. Online coin clubs are growing. Convenience is one reason.

Mail-order coin and exonumia buying is fast and convenient. Reputable periodicals will refuse ads from companies known to be fraudulent or inadequate in the area of customer service, although they cannot do a perfect job of screening. When you are starting out, it is best to use those companies that have a long-term successful relationship with the periodical they are advertising with. Follow the directions in the ad exactly for fastest service. Make sure you include adequate postage fees. If you have a special request, write or call to inquire. Almost all mail-order companies are happy to tackle any wish list.

Those same magazines and newspapers will carry ads from local coin clubs and for upcoming shows and conventions. Check the calendar area for dates and times. Coin shows and coin conventions can be a lot of fun because you are among like-minded souls. Ask around at the bourse (the area with the tables and booths set up by coin dealers) for sellers and attendees who specialize in lucky items. And don't forget to check the schedule for any presentations or seminars that might relate to your specialty.

The annual convention of the American Numismatic Association (ANA; *www.money.org*) is an unforgettable event for any kind of coin collector. In addition to the opportunities for buying (and trading), there are presentations, exhibits, and seminars.

SECURITY MEANS AWARENESS

It is a sad fact but it is not uncommon for thieves to target people leaving coin shows and estate auctions after coins and banknotes have been sold. These items are relatively small and are easy to fence. Don't be a victim.

When you leave any place that sells coins or other valuable collectibles, even if you purchased nothing, make sure there are plenty of people in the parking lot. If no one is around, ask a security guard to accompany you to your parking space. Be aware of your surroundings. If anyone appears to be lurking or hiding, go and get a security guard or police officer.

Once in your car, make a mental note of any cars that follow you out of the parking lot. Check again after a mile or two, and if you see that same car in your rearview mirror, drive to the nearest police station. If that car follows you there, lean on your horn or stay on your cell phone with 911 until an officer emerges.

Thieves will smash a window or pry open your trunk in seconds if they think there is a briefcase of coins or currency there. In short, you should always act as if a thief is nearby to avoid becoming the victim of one.

ESTATE SALES, LIVE AUCTIONS, FLEA MARKETS, AND YARD SALES

If you like the idea of finding buried treasure, you'll probably enjoy buying lucky coins and medals at live sales and flea markets. Stories are told and retold of people purchasing jars of coins and old Whitman penny folders at yard and estate sales and finding rarities within.

If you attend a live auction or an estate sale, here are a few tips:

- Take your favorite price guides along in case you have to look up something. Since these books can be heavy, you can leave them in the car. Then simply jot down information about the items you wish to look up and go back to your car before the auction to do a bit of research.
- Arrive early so you can look over coin and token collections before the bidding starts.
- You may have to buy items you don't want in order to get items you do within the same lot. Make sure that the time and trouble of selling the unwanted items is worth it to you.
- Keep a poker face while bidding lest the people bidding against you decide that your enthusiasm indicates a valuable item in the group.
- Decide in advance what your maximum price is and stick to it. Don't allow the excitement of the bidding to go to your head.

At yard sales, look for cigar boxes, jelly jars, sugar canisters, and tins full of coins, medals, or tokens. These collections often span decades and might produce some very interesting lucky items. Ask about advertising and World's Fair tokens that have good-luck messages. Check lots made up of world coins for lucky French angels, Chinese cash coins, and dragon coins. You could find almost anything in these groups.

Coin and exonumia sellers at flea markets will be selling individual items, definitely worth the time it takes to stop and look. Pay extra close attention to any box they may have where you can choose as many items as you want for a set price. There could be some winners at the bottom of that box!

It may sound obvious but it bears stressing: Never toss out anything simply because it looks common or uninteresting or because nothing is known about it. You could be throwing out something valuable. This writer once met a man who made such a mistake, and it cost him a small fortune.

He had been refurbishing an old house he bought. In one corner of the attic, he found a small dusty box with a wad of paper money inside. It appeared to be Confederate currency, but he seriously doubted its authenticity. The paper was thin and flimsy and the colors drab. It looked like play money. He put one of the bills into his wallet to keep as a souvenir and threw the rest away.

When he described his "phony find" to me months later, I encouraged him to have the surviving note appraised because genuine Confederate currency often looks like play money. The South did not have the funds to create sophisticated currency. Banknotes were printed on whatever paper was at hand, especially near the end of the war.

He took it to a coin dealer who declared his $50 Rebel shinplaster to be genuine. A *shinplaster* is so called because the decline in the value of Rebel money made it fit only for uses such as a shin plaster. It was worth ten times its face value in modern-day Yankee dollars! That big wad of "worthless paper" he had thrown away was surely worth several thousand dollars.

LUCKY POCKET CHANGE

One place where collectible coins can be found for face value that many people overlook is the local bank. Your bank can supply you with banknotes, which you can search for lucky 8s and 7s, rolls of coins, which you can search for key dates, tokens, and medals.

Searching rolls is a fun hobby, both fascinating and easy to enjoy. Simply visit different banks; purchase rolls of coins at face value; search them for key dates, mint errors, and filler tokens (inexpensive tokens that some people place into coin rolls to take up space); and return to the bank those coins you do not wish to keep.

Recently, a friend bought every Kennedy half-dollar that her local bank acquired over a period of six months, in order to search the rolls. She was able to build a 90 percent full collection of dates and found an average of one silver half-dollar in each roll that she searched. This circulated collection was worth significantly more than the face value of the coins alone.

Searching bank rolls can yield some amazing finds, for instance:

- rare and potentially valuable error coins, such as a coin struck with a rotated die, a doubled-die coin, or one struck off-center
- tokens and small medals mixed into the rolls, including vintage lucky tokens
- older U.S. dimes, quarters, and halves struck before the mid-1960s and containing some silver content
- silver war nickels made during World War II
- world coins of similar size or metal content mixed in with the U.S. coins, some of which might depict lucky animals or themes
- rare date or key date coins in a series

RARE COINS DO ENTER CIRCULATION

Finding silver and key date coins occurs more often than you might think. A collector or family member may spend one by mistake, but there are two not so uncommon situations that place the most key date coins back into circulation.

The first is when a coin collector dies without leaving instructions for his or her heirs about how to properly sell a coin collection. The heirs might assume the old pennies and other minor coins aren't worth anything and take them down to the bank to trade for paper money. Or they may cash in the glass jar full of old quarters. This is a costly error, for there are U.S. coin dates in all denominations that are quite rare and valuable.

The second situation occurs when thieves steal a coin collection and don't realize what they have. They may try to fence a silver dollar or banknote collection but assume that the minor denomination coins are only worth their face value. They'll discard or spend these anywhere.

Because rare coins do sometimes find their way back into circulation, you should always glance at your pocket change before spending it. You never know what you'll find. Recently, a coin magazine reported the story of a man who took a penny from one of those little bowls at a convenience store cash register marked "Leave a penny, take a penny." The Lincoln cent turned out to be a rare find worth more than $100.

PUBLICATIONS

If you don't have some idea of rarity and value before you buy, you will spend more than necessary, and you will never know the full story behind the coins or tokens. The publications listed in this section are designed to save you time, money, and frustration.

Books

Since coin and exonumia catalog price guides have a smaller audience than other types of references, they tend to be somewhat expensive. If you don't require the latest edition, check your local thrift store or secondhand bookstore for a used copy. You can also go online to Web sites that sell used books at reasonable prices, like Amazon.com and Half.com. For example, a recent check of one used book site uncovered a set of three of the most comprehensive paper money price guides available, for $30 delivered. They were four-year-old ex-library copies in excellent condition that had originally come from a library book sale. New, these telephone-book-sized volumes would have cost more than $150.

There are three types of books listed in the following pages: the large standard numismatic references, the specialized titles, and books about luck. The standard references are the books you use to look up a certain coin, medal, or token to learn about its current value, how many were produced, and other pertinent facts, such as weight and diameter. The specialty books explore a specific area of numismatics that lucky coins will overlap, like U.S. tokens, or a related topic, such as detecting counterfeit coins.

Standard References on Coins and Paper Money

Bruce, Colin R., II, and Neil Shafer. *Standard Catalog of World Paper Money.* Volume I: *Specialized Issues,* 8th Edition. Volume II: *General Issues,* 9th Edition. Volume III: *Modern Issues, 1961–2001,* 7th Edition. Iola, Wisconsin: Krause Publications, 2001.

Updated regularly, this is the indispensable three-part guide for collectors of world paper money. Krause also publishes a comprehensive U.S. paper money price guide that contains more information than can be provided about U.S. currency in the world guides.

Hudgeons, Marc, and Tom. *The Official Blackbook Price Guide to World Coins, 9th Edition.* New York: Random House, 2005.

The Official Blackbook series of small paperbacks also includes issues for U.S. coins and paper money. These are not as comprehensive as the Red Book and the Standard Catalog series, but they offer a good, economical introduction to collecting. They are also handy to take with you when you visit coin conventions, coin shops, and estate sales.

Krause, Chester L., and Clifford Mishler. *2006 Standard Catalog of World Coins, 1901–Present.* Edited by Colin R. Bruce, II. Iola, Wisconsin: Krause Publications, 2005.

Updated annually, this standard reference covers the most recent full century in one volume and earlier centuries in other volumes. With its illustrations and specifications, it is an absolute must for the world coin collector.

Yeoman, R. S. *The Official Red Book: A Guide Book of United States Coins*, 57th Edition. Edited by Kenneth Bressett. Atlanta: Whitman Coin Publishers, 2003.
This popular guide to U.S. coins provides a brief overview of the history of U.S. coinage, retail prices, mintage figures, grading information, and much more. Some call the *Red Book* "the bible of U.S. coin collecting."

Numismatic Specialty Books

Alpert, Stephen P. *Large Lucky Souvenir Coins*. Los Angeles: Stephen P. Alpert, 1979.
This slender illustrated volume is very helpful for the collector of three-inch-diameter lucky penny medals.

Alpert, Stephen P., and Lawrence E. Elman. *Tokens and Medals: A Guide to the Identification and Values of United States Exonumia*. Los Angeles: Stephen P. Alpert, 1991.
Trade, tax, amusement, advertising, vending, and many other types of tokens are discussed in this helpful book. The authors examine some of the more obscure tokens and medals that other books overlook.

Anderson, Shane M. *The Complete Lincoln Cent Encyclopedia*. Iola, Wisconsin: Krause Publications, 1996.
This is a slender but fascinating and detailed overview of the beloved American penny, our native lucky coin.

Bruce, Colin R., II. *Unusual World Coins*. Iola, Wisconsin: Krause Publications, 1992.
This helpful resource for the more obscure noncirculating world coins and medallic issues is out of print, but you can still find copies at used book stores and online.

Clain-Stefanelli, Elvira, and Vladimir Clain-Stefanelli. *The Beauty and Lore of Coins, Currency and Medals*. Croton-on-Hudson, New York: Riverwood Publishers, 1974.
This excellent review of the history of numismatic collectibles features wonderful illustrations.

Coin World Almanac. Sidney, Ohio: Amos Press, 2000.
The staff of *Coin World* offer this superb overall guide to coin and paper money collecting with a wealth of useful information, from detecting fakes to storing coins properly.

Fivaz, Bill. *Helpful Hints for Enjoying Coin Collecting.* Savannah, Georgia: Stanton Printing & Publishing, 1999.
This comprehensive book was written by a man with fifty years of experience in coin collecting. He shares a great deal of basic information with the goal of making the hobby fun for all. Especially helpful are sections on the basic grading of coins, recommended reading suggestions, and a list of specialty coin clubs.

Jen, David. *Chinese Cash: Identification and Price Guide.* Iola, Wisconsin: Krause Publications, 2000.
Two thousand illustrations in this very helpful volume mean that you don't have to be able to read Chinese to be able to identify your cash coins by date and mintmark.

Jones, Mark. *The Art of the Medal.* London: British Museum Publications Limited, 1979.
This beautifully illustrated book offers fine reading on the history and making of medals.

Krause, Chester L. *Guidebook of Franklin Mint Issues.* Iola, Wisconsin: Krause Publications, 1978.
The bad news is that this helpful reference about Franklin Mint coins, medals, and tokens is out of print. The good news is that older copies of different editions are available on many online auction sites and at used book stores. The book presents all of the specifications for most of the numismatic issues of this once prolific private mint.

Rulau, Russell. *Standard Catalog of United States Tokens, 1700–1900,* 2nd Edition. Iola, Wisconsin: Krause Publications, 1997.
For tokens made prior to 1900, this is a must-have reference book.

Books About Luck

Ashley, Leonard R. N. *The Complete Book of Superstition, Prophecy and Luck*. London: Robson Books, 1984.

Fitzgerald, Randall. *Lucky You! Proven Strategies You Can Use to Find Your Fortune*. New York: Citadel, 2004.

Levinson, Horace C. *Chance, Luck and Statistics*. Mineola, New York: Dover, 2001.

Rescher, Nicholas. *Luck: The Brilliant Randomness of Everyday Life*. Pittsburgh: University of Pittsburgh, 2001.

Wiseman, Richard. *The Luck Factor: Changing Your Luck, Changing Your Life, the Four Essential Principles*. New York: Hyperion, 2003.

FAQs, Articles, Magazines, and Newsletters

FAQs

In the early days of the Internet, people new to discussion areas usually asked the exact same questions about the topic. To save time answering the same questions over and over, someone came up with the idea of writing a brief introduction answering these common questions. The frequently asked questions (FAQ) file was born. There are thousands of FAQs on the Internet today on every conceivable topic, including collecting coins and paper money.

Coin Collecting FAQ, http://www.telesphere.com/ts/coins/faq.html (maintained by Chuck D'Ambra Coins) offers a terrific introduction that addresses all of the most-asked questions about coin collecting. If it does not have the answer to your question, chances are it tells you where to find the answer.

Paper Money Collecting FAQ, http://www.faqs.org/faqs/coin-collecting/paper-money-faq/preamble.html (currently maintained by Bruce Giese) is another informative and time-saving tool.

Articles

Andrew, John. "Lucky Pennies Work, But Only in the Mind." *Coin World* (February 9, 2004), p. 65.

"Captain's 'Lucky Coin' Found in Civil War Submarine." *National Geographic News* (May 2001), http://news.nationalgeographic.com/news/2001/05/0524_hunleycoin.html.

"Dixon's Love Token," www.thehunley.com.

Tebben, Gerald. "Sixpence in Shoe Is Still a Custom." *Columbus Dispatch* (February 2000).

Zoroya, Gregg. "Doomed Civil War Sailor's Lucky Coin Goes on Display." *USA Today* (February 26, 2002), www.usatoday.com/life/2002/2002-02-27-soldier.htm.

Coin and Numismatic Print Magazines

Coin collectors love their hobby. They love to talk about it, write about it, and read about it. Coin and currency collecting periodicals abound for this reason. It's a good idea to try sample copies of several before deciding which ones warrant a subscription. Here is a partial list:

Bank Note Reporter, www.collect.com/interest/periodical.asp?Pub=BR. Bank Note Reporter, Krause Publications, 700 E. State St., Iola, WI 54990. Krause (www.krause.com/static/coins.htm) also publishes these magazines: *Numismatic News*, *World Coin News*, *Coins Magazine*, and *Coin Prices*.

COINage, www.coinagemag.com. *COINage*, Miller Magazines, 4880 Market Street, Ventura, CA 93003.

Coin World, www.coinworld.com. *Coin World*, P.O. Box 150, Sidney, OH 45365-0150. Subscriptions: 800-253-4555. Also publishes *Coin Values* magazine (a price guide for U.S. coins) and a quarterly called *Paper Money Values*.

Error Trends Coin Magazine, www.etcmmag.com. *Error Trends Coin Magazine*, P.O. Box 158, Oceanside, NY 11572-0158. Phone: 516-764-8063.

The Numismatist, www.money.org. *The Numismatist*, American Numismatic Association, 818 N. Cascade Ave., Colorado Springs, CO 80903-3279. Membership: 800-514-2646. The ANA also publishes *YN* (*Your Newsletter*), an e-zine.

E-Zines (Electronic Magazines and Newsletters)

Coin Connoisseur, www.coinconnoisseur.com.

Coin Resource, www.coinresource.com.

CoinWeek, www.coinweek.com.

Numismatic Literary Guild newsletter, www.numismaticliteraryguild.org.

SOCIALIZING WITH EXPERTS AND OTHER COLLECTORS

Coin collectors as a whole enjoy socializing with other coin collectors and helping beginners, especially kids. Many coin fanciers purposely spend the less well-known U.S. currency types (e.g., two-dollar bills; Eisenhower, Susan B. Anthony, and Sacagawea dollar coins; and Kennedy half-dollars) in everyday transactions in order to publicize their existence. When a new coin design is released, they rush to mark the date that one first showed up in pocket change. Some collectors fill display cases at public libraries to educate the public about the history behind a certain type of money.

Whether learning, sharing, or both, there are six major socializing and educational opportunities for numismatists of all kinds. These are the American Numismatic Association, clubs, shows, public meetings of the Citizens Coinage Advisory Committee, online bulletin boards, and chat rooms.

American Numismatic Association

If you are ever in Colorado Springs, Colorado, consider a trip to the American Numismatic Association (ANA). This nonprofit educational organization maintains a library, a museum, a schedule of classes, and an informative Web site; hosts a famous annual convention; and publishes an interesting magazine, *The Numismatist*. Membership information is available by calling 800-514-2646.

The membership fee pays for *The Numismatist*, but many collectors see another major value in that fee. If you find yourself in the middle of a transaction gone bad, and if the seller is an ANA member, the ANA will mediate the dispute.

Clubs and Shows

What are clubs and shows like? Club meetings are watering holes for coin hobbyists. A typical meeting may feature a guest speaker or a specific topic, coin exhibits, buy and sell opportunities, snacks or a meal, or a combination of the above. The only way to find out if your local coin club members share your collecting passion is to attend a meeting or two.

Coin shows and conventions are similar to coin clubs but greatly expanded. Some of the larger shows may have dozens of tables set up in the bourse, where the sellers sell and the buyers buy for an entire weekend. There will be opportunities to meet and talk to numismatic writers and hear detailed presentations from experts in the field. The annual money show of the ANA is the ultimate coin show for most collectors. It is held each year in a different major city.

All print numismatic magazines and some of the electronic ones publish lists of coin clubs and coin shows. You can sometimes also find information about them in the community calendar section of the local newspaper.

An easy way to see a nationwide list of clubs and upcoming events is at the ANA Web site. Membership is optional in order to access this information.

The ANA's shows and conventions page is *www.money.org/conventiondept.html*. The ANA's clubs page, *www.money.org/clublist.html*, contains several lists of coin clubs: national, regional, by state, international, and by specialty.

If you want to start a local or online lucky coin club, the ANA Web site offers a form you can use to register your new club. Since club lists, addresses, and meeting schedules change frequently, it is wise to contact someone in the club before attending a meeting. If a trip to the Web site is not feasible, the ANA can be reached by letter, phone call, or fax: American Numismatic Association, 818 N. Cascade

Ave., Colorado Springs, CO 80903-3279; main phone: 719-632-2646, membership: 800-514-2646, general: 800-367-9723, fax: 719-634-4085.

Public Meetings of the Citizens Coinage Advisory Committee

The Citizens Coinage Advisory Committee is one of two national committees that review proposed coinage and medallic design for the U.S. government and then make recommendations to the Secretary of the Treasury. (The Commission of Fine Arts, www.cfa.gov, is the other one.) The CCAC is made up of volunteer citizens. It usually meets in Washington, D.C., approximately every other month but also holds meetings in cities where there is a branch of the U.S. Mint (e.g., Denver, San Francisco, or Philadelphia) or the city hosting the annual ANA convention.

The public meetings of the CCAC represent an opportunity to meet other folks interested in coins and medals and to hear people from varied backgrounds (history professor, art expert, numismatist, etc.) discuss coin design and the history behind each proposal. You can find out more by visiting the Web site of the CCAC (*www.ccac.gov*); or of the U.S. Mint pressroom (*www.usmint.gov/pressroom*). You can also visit these same Web sites to apply to serve a six-year term on the CCAC.

Online Message Boards and Live Chats

An online message board is simply a group discussion in which participants use a computer keyboard to type messages and replies instead of actually speaking to one another. Message boards differ from online chats only in their immediacy. With a message board, typed messages are left to be read and replied to by other members at a later time, exactly the way you might thumbtack a paper message to a cork bulletin board. A chat is a live discussion in real time where people are communicating directly with each other through their keyboards. Some people prefer the relaxed nature of a message board, while others thrive on the more frenetic pace of the chat room.

Message Boards

Coin Talk Numismatic Discussion Forum, www.cointalk.org

This is a very popular message board dealing with a wide variety of coin-related topics. As with other message boards, if you don't see a thread (discussion topic) worth joining, you can start a new topic.

eBay Coins & Paper Money Discussion Board, http://forums.ebay.com

This message board was created specifically for members of the eBay Coin & Paper Money community, the buyers and sellers. People who post have to be registered eBay members, and they must follow the rules of the message board. These rules include things like no advertising, no profanity, and no criticism of specifically named eBay members. The purpose of the message board is to allow members to socialize, trade tips, find answers, and the like. (To access, go to *www.ebay.com* and click "Community" at the top of the page. Then click "Discussion Boards," then click "Coins & Paper Money.")

Collectors Universe Forums, http://forums.collectors.com

Collectors Universe is a large company made up of small companies that sell all types of collectibles, including coins. Several of their popular, easy-to-use message boards are just for numismatic people. U.S. coins, world coins, tokens—any topic is fine.

U.S. Coin Collectors Trading Post Message Board, http://groups.msn.com/USCoinCollectorsTradingPost/opendiscussion.msnw

This is one of the MSN discussion groups. As with other message boards, there are some common-sense rules. This one features a topic where you can describe items for sale and another topic for world coin fanciers. The MSN coin chat is available by subscription only.

Chat Rooms

About Coin Collecting Chat, http://coins.about.com/mpchat.htm

About.com is a massive Web site with many topics "about" almost anything you can think of, including hobbies. This chat room is affiliated with About's stamp and coin collecting page.

eBay Chat: Coins & Paper Money,
http://chatboards.ebay.com/chat.jsp?forum=1&thread=27

The chat room complements the discussion board of the same topic on eBay. The chat room also has live discussions. It is simple to switch back and forth between the message boards and chat rooms, if needed. Don't be intimidated by some of the jargon. The people posting will be happy to explain the wording of any post if you ask. After a few sessions, you will feel quite comfortable talking to the other collectors. (Go to *www.ebay.com* and click "Community" on the top of the page. Then click "Chat Rooms," then click "Coins and Paper Money.")

MARKET TRENDS AND PRICE GUIDE

Good luck is often with the person who
does not include it in his plans

—Anonymous

It is said that the value of any coin is the amount that someone is willing to pay for it. While this is true, buyers get more bang for their buck when they are aware of estimated values for the items they want.

These pages are an overview of current prices for various items within the major categories of lucky coin collecting. These do not include values for the rarest dates or varieties within a series. For example, the range listed for common Chinese cash coins is $2 to $10 each. Not mentioned is the fact that there are hundreds of scarce varieties, some of which sell for many thousands of dollars.

These values can only estimate a range because mintage figures are not available for most privately made lucky tokens and medals. Furthermore, there are too many variables for exact amounts to be reliable. For example, with a U.S. silver dime love token, the final value will be affected by the date, the condition of the obverse, the nature of the message (those inscribed to Mom are more popular than those with a specific set of initials, for example), the price of silver, and the intricacy and artistic merit of the reverse side engraving.

In evaluating unaltered legal tender coins, there is much more precision than there can be with altered items and exonumia. Using an older price guide for more common items is fine, but for the pricier coins, it is best to refer to an up-to-date price sheet, magazine, or current year values catalog. Prices will rise more because they continue to increase in rarity over time on the more expensive items and those in like-new condition.

Why Rare Coins Become More Rare

Scarce uncirculated items rise in value faster because such pieces can and do become more rare. Barring the discovery of a hoard of uncirculated examples, they cannot become more plentiful. For example, 334,705 silver Japanese "lucky dragon" 50 sen coins were made in the key date year of 1908. This is a relatively small number, and this type of coin is obsolete (i.e., it will never be made again). In uncirculated condition, the KM (Krause and Mishler) catalog price guide value is $500. This drops substantially to $150 if the coin is handled or slightly circulated, a condition called XF (extra fine).

Logically, the number of uncirculated coins of this or any rare type must decline to some degree over time. Some specimens may be:

- damaged by exposure to the elements
- lost to fire, flood, storm, or earthquake
- stolen
- hidden for safety but never found
- melted in times of economic distress or if silver prices increase dramatically
- originally considered to be authentic but later found to be counterfeit
- handled to the extent that they no longer grade uncirculated

Such circumstances will always decrease the finite number of uncirculated examples but slightly increase the number of XF coins. Therefore, over time, the value of the more and more scarce uncirculated issues is likely to go up more than the slightly increased number of XF specimens, simply because of scarcity.

This process affects XF coins, too, of course, as some of these may grade only very fine (VF) or fine (F) due to the ravages of time. Unlike uncirculated coins, however, the loss of some XF grades will be somewhat replenished by the addition of a few new XF grades, coins that were formerly uncirculated. This gradual process means that the truly pristine coins can only become more scarce and thus more valuable.

Altered Lucky Coins

Love Tokens, U.S. Dimes
Seated Liberty, $5 to $50
Barber, $5 to $40
Mercury, $5 to $35

Love Tokens, British Sixpence
Victorian (prior to 1902), $15 to $65
Silver (prior to 1947), $10 to $40
Enameled, $20 to $75
Love Token, Hunley Civil War Token Replica, $10 to $30

U.S. Hobo Nickels
Buffalo, $5 to $150
Jefferson, $5 to $50

Encased Cents
U.S. and Canada, $1 to $20
Other Nations, $2 to $30
Rolled (elongated) Cents, $1 to $25

Large 3" Lucky Penny/Nickel Medallions
White Metal, $3 to $10
Bronze, $4 to $30

Other U.S. Good-Luck Tokens

Advertising
Pre–WWII, $10 to $32
Post–WWII, $2 to $24
Franklin Mint Bronze Advertising, $4 to $14

Billiken
Brass, Bronze, or Copper, $9 to $27
Silver, $28 to $40

Casino
Silver Strikes, $11 to $38
Casino Chips, $2 to $175
Children's Pocket Pieces, $2.50 to $9
Good-Fors, $1 to $12
Lucky Lindy Tokens, $4 to $8
Military Challenge Coins
Bronze, $3 to $15
Bronze Enameled, $7 to $25
Nonprofit and Religious, $5 to $33
Political, Military, and War, $6 to $48
Super Bowl Coin Toss Silver Replicas, $14 to $40

Lucky World Tokens and Charms
Austria, New Year Frog Tokens, $5 to $21
Germany and Canada, Encased Cents, $4 to $15
Korea, Charms, $9 to $75

Lucky World Coins

China

Cash Coins, $2 to $10

Bronze and Copper Dragon Coins, $3 to $20

Boy with Carp, 1997 5 Yuan, Gold, $35 to $50

France, Angel Coin Silver, 100 Francs, $30 to $40

Ireland, Hen Penny, $2 to $40

Japan, Cash Coins, $4 to $20

Laos, 2003 15,000 Kip, Flower Horn Fish Silver Proof, $45 to $55

Liberia, Elephants

Half Cent, $0.50 to $2

Penny, $0.50 to $6

Two Cents, $0.50 to $7

Five Cents, $0.50 to $2

Liberia, Y2K Coins

Chinese Zodiac, 2000 $5 Copper-Nickel Coins, $3 to $5 each

"Luckiest Coin," 2000 $10 (colorized by AHS), $15 to $24

Lucky Sixpence

Great Britain, $1 to $200

Other Commonwealth Nations, $3 to $35

Other Lucky World Items

Franklin Mint Lucky Medal Collection (12 medals)

Bronze, $35 to $60

Silver, $60 to $120

American Historic Society, Lucky Coin Collection (25 coins), $12 to $25

Lucky Paper Money and Prosperity Notes

U.S. Paper Money, One Dollar

Four or More Consecutive 8s in Serial Number, $4 to $8

Four or More Consecutive 7s in Serial Number, $3 to $7

World Banknotes

Four or More Consecutive 7s or 8s in Serial Number, $1 to $8

A Serial Number Made Up Entirely of a Single Digit, $10 to $395

Million-Dollar Notes, $0.50 to $2

Lucky Hell Note Set, Different Denominations, $1 to $10

Chinese New Year Set with Paper Money, Coin, Medal, $10 to $17

COMMON ACRONYMS AND ABBREVIATIONS IN COIN COLLECTING

I am a great believer in luck, and I find the harder I work the more I have of it.

—Thomas Jefferson

An abbreviation is simply a shortcut of some kind for a word or group of words, such as *unc* for *uncirculated*. An acronym is a type of abbreviation that is also a word itself, such as FUN, the acronym of Florida United Numismatists. Coin and exonumia collecting has many abbreviations and acronyms. This section will list some of the common ones. If you don't find the one you want here, try the Acronym Finder (*www.acronymfinder.com*), a searchable Web site featuring more than 342,000 acronyms and abbreviations on many topics.

AG—About good, a coin grade or an opinion regarding condition. In a grading hierarchy of BU, UNC, AU, XF (or EF), VF, F, VG, G, and AG, AG is the coin in the poorest condition of all.

ANA—American Numismatic Association.

AU—About (or almost) uncirculated, a coin grade or an opinion regarding condition.

BU—Brilliant uncirculated—the best of the uncirculated, a coin grade or an opinion regarding condition.

BV—Bullion value.

CW—Coin World, a coin collecting publication.

D—Denver (Colorado) mintmark.

EF (also called XF)—Extra fine, a coin grade or an opinion regarding condition.

F—Fine, a coin grade or an opinion regarding condition.

FAQ—Frequently asked question, an Internet phrase.

G—Good, a coin grade or an opinion regarding condition.

KM#—Krause and Mishler number, from the *Standard Catalog of World Coins*.

MS—Mint state, an uncirculated, pristine coin in the same condition as when it left the mint.

ND—No date.

NLG—Numismatic Literary Guild, an organization of writers of numismatic articles and books.

NN—*Numismatic News*, a coin collecting publication.

P—Philadelphia (Pennsylvania) mintmark.

PF—Proof, the rarest and most costly type of coin strike, often featuring frosted cameos and mirrored fields on the same coin.

PL—Prooflike, similar to a proof finish. See PF.

PVC—Polyvinyl chloride, contamination from a soft plastic coin holder that ruins the surface of coins and medals.

S—San Francisco (California) mintmark.

UNC—Uncirculated, a coin grade or an opinion regarding condition.

VF—Very fine, a coin grade or an opinion regarding condition.

VG—Very good, a coin grade or an opinion regarding condition.

W—West Point (New York) mintmark.

XF (also called EF)—Extra fine, a coin grade or an opinion regarding condition.

GLOSSARY

A pound of pluck is worth a ton of luck!

—*James A. Garfield*

album
A book with plastic-covered portholes for coin storage.

altered coin
A coin or coinlike object that has been intentionally modified (e.g., gold-plated or colorized) after the minting process. Can also refer to the alteration of a mintmark for deceptive purposes.

bag marks
Small scratches caused by coins making contact in mint bags. Also known as contact marks.

banknote
Paper money issued by or through a bank.

bosen coins
The "mother coins" from which a batch of cash coins is created. Bosens are highly valued for their sharper than average detail.

Bureau of Engraving and Printing (BEP)
The agency of the U.S. Treasury Department that produces paper money.

certified coin
A coin that has been identified, authenticated, and graded by a coin grading service.

coin
Legal tender metal.

commemorative
A coin or medal with a design that commemorates a person, a place, a thing, or an event.

contact marks
Small scratches caused by coins making contact in mint bags. Also known as bag marks.

counterfeit
An imitation of legal tender made for fraudulent purposes.

cull
A coin that is so badly worn that the words, the numbers, and at least part of the design are not discernible.

denomination
The face value (e.g., ten cents) of a coin.

edge
Called the third side of a coin, this is where you should place your fingers when holding a coin.

error
Any unintentional mistake made during the minting process that creates coins and medals that do not appear to be made correctly.

exonumia
Tokens, medals, medallic charms, and other nonlegal tender coinlike objects.

flip
A plastic holder normally used for a single coin. Also called a 2x2.

folder
A coin holder consisting of trifold cardboard with enough depression to mount coins; made for coins of a specific series (e.g., a folder of Mercury dimes).

grading
A process of determining the quality of a coin's condition using words or word-number combinations—from best to worst: brilliant uncirculated (BU), uncirculated (UNC), about uncirculated (AU), extra fine (XF or EF), very fine (VF), fine (F), very good (VG), good (G), about good (AG), and cull (completely worn). Numbers range from 4 to 70. common letter and number combinations include: MS (UNC) 60 to 70, AU 50 to 58, XF 40 to 45, VF 20 to 35, F 12, V 8 to 10, and G 4 to 6.

groat
Slang for a British fourpence, or 4p.

incuse
Concave, a design element that is cut into the metal instead of being raised above it.

key date
The scarcest and most expensive member or members of a coin series.

legal tender
Money that is authorized by a government as payable for debts.

legend
Lettering or wording on a coin (e.g., "In God We Trust").

loupe
A type of small magnifying glass used by numismatists and jewelers.

lucky pocket piece
Coin, medal, or token carried in a pocket and purported to bring good luck.

medal or medallion
A coinlike object struck to commemorate a person, a place, a thing, or an event.

mule
A coin struck from two dies not intended to be used together, such as a coin with a dollar obverse and a quarter reverse.

numismatist
A person who collects and/or studies numismatic items (e.g., coins, tokens, medals, and paper money).

obverse
The front, or "heads," side of a coin.

pattern
A coin struck as a test piece for a new design of legal tender. Also called essai and proba.

reverse
The back, or "tails," side of a coin.

slab
A plastic case in which professionally graded coins are sealed to protect them from the elements and preserve their condition.

spinner
A token made with a small bump in the center on which the token can be spun with a flick of the wrist. An arrow on the token points to the luckiest person present when the spinner stops spinning.

token
A coinlike object, many of which can be traded for a service or for goods.

toning
Color or darkening acquired from a coin's exposure to air over a long period of time.

type set
A set of coins collected because of a common denominator (e.g., one of each denomination of coin ever made by the United States, one of each type of sixpence ever minted by Commonwealth nations, and pennies of the world).

uncirculated
Never circulated, a new-looking coin or medal.

world coins
In the United States, "world coins" refer to non-U.S. coins.

INDEX

True luck consists not in holding the best of the cards at the table; luckiest is he who knows just when to rise and go home.

—John Hay, 1838–1905

Page numbers in italics refer to illustrations and captions.